~ LEADING ~
KINGDOM MOVEMENTS

the "Everyman" notebook on how to change the world

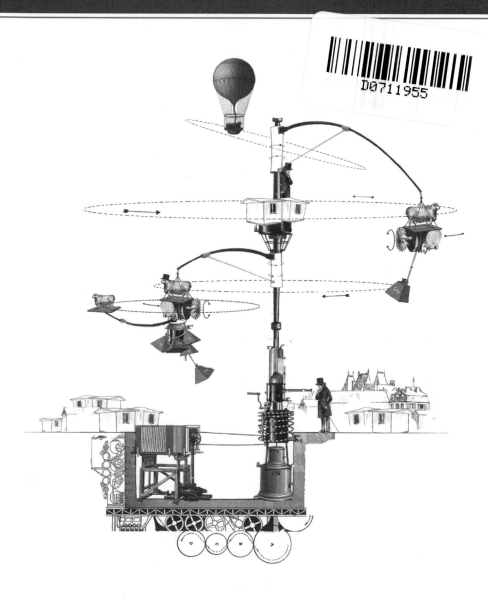

Mike Breen and the 3DM Team

Leading Kingdom Movements
© Copyright 2013 by Mike Breen

First printing 2013
Printed in Myrtle Beach, SC @ Sheriar Press
4 5 6 7 8 9 10 11 12 13 Printing/Year 15 14 13 12 11 10

Cover Design: Blake Berg
Editor/Interior Design: Pete Berg
ISBN: 978-0-9846643-6-8

DEDICATION

This book is dedicated to everyone who is part of The Order of Mission. In almost every way imaginable, all I'm doing in this book is telling the history of the Kingdom movement in which we find ourselves. It is the great honor of my life to serve with you.

CREDITS

Author	**Mike Breen**
Writer	**Doug Paul**
Editors	**Robert Neely**
	Ben Sternke
	Terry Hofecker
Design	**Blake Berg**
	Pete Berg
Production	**Libby Culmer**

Support

Beccy Beresic	**Kimberly Berg**
Julie Bird	**Sally Breen**
Sam Breen	**Taylor Breen**
Craig Cheney	**Judy Cheney**
Gavin Culmer	**Angela Davila**
Anthony Davila	**Si Ford**
Joan Gooley	**Jessie Harrelson**
Elizabeth Paul	**Eric Pfeiffer**
Kandi Pfeiffer	**Jo Rapps**
Kevin Rapps	**Courtney Reichley**
David Reichley	**Dave Rhodes**
Kim Rhodes	**Brandon Schaefer**
T.J. Schaefer	**Deb Sternke**
Patty Wyngaard	**Peter Wyngaard**

⌁ ABOUT THE COVER ART ⌁

I've always been fascinated with how things work. My favorite childhood toys were the ones I would put together myself: legos, blocks, models, potato clock. I had the game *Mousetrap*, but I never actually played the game. I just assembled all the parts and set the contraption into action — flip the man in the pan, the trap is set, NOW DROP THE NET!

But I'm not just concerned with how things work. I want to know *why* they work the way they do. What are the concepts and theories behind their functionality? *Why* do levers and inclined planes make work easier? *Why* does the man flip in the pan? *Why* is a white car cooler in the summer? How can I change the world?

Change the world. That seems daunting. It's great to be able to hook up my TV or to fix a leaking sink, but now we are getting into issues of life and death—life abundant and death eternal. But can the mechanics of these issues be understood like anything else? If there *were* a machine that lead Kingdom movements, what would it look like? How would it work? Where are the moving parts? Why does it work the way it does? What are the theories, concepts, and theologies that guide it?

I'm certainly not saying that the Kingdom of God can be casually reduced down to a simple machine. But, I am saying that the more fully I understand the "moving parts" and how I fit into them, the more fully I can step into the life I was created to live. The more I understand the "machine", the better I can maintain it. I can operate it more efficiently, and I can effortlessly adapt it to any situation.

Give a man a fish and he can eat for a day, but teach a man to fish and he can eat for a lifetime. Changing the world may not be so daunting after all.

Blake Berg
Cover designer

TABLE OF CONTENTS

Introduction v

Part 1: The Age of Earthquakes

Chapter 1:
In the Rubble of the Earthquake. 3

Part 2: My Story

Chapter 2:
The Breaking 27

Chapter 3:
The Spirit 37

Chapter 4:
Grace and Faith 45

Chapter 5:
The Multiplication Years 69

Chapter 6:
The Two Towers Fall 79

Part 3: The Journey Within

Chapter 7:
Paul: A Man with a Mission 91

Chapter 8:
Paul: Message 103

Chapter 9:
Paul: Method 117

Chapter 10:
Paul: Miraculous + Movement 139

Chapter 11:
Navigating the Spiritual Terrain. 157

Part 4: The Mechanics of a Movement

Chapter 12:
Orbital Patterns, Higgs Boson, and Molasses 169

Chapter 13:
Red-hot Centers. 183

Part 5: The Conclusion

Chapter 14:
To Ephesus and Beyond. 201

A BRIEF NOTE ~ ABOUT THIS BOOK ~ BEFORE READING

Although this is a stand-alone book, it falls within a trajectory of content that the 3DM content team and I have crafted for the teams of people who engage in our two-year Learning Community process. This particular book serves as the fourth and final book of this series.

Our core books, following the trajectory of the Learning Communities, each build on the content established in the previous books. They are the following:

- Building a Discipling Culture
- Multiplying Missional Leaders
- Launching Missional Communities
- Leading Kingdom Movements

Because of this approach, what appears to be "insider language" may show up from time to time as I reference points made in the previous books. However, I believe we've made a concerted effort to explain these points so this book can stand on its own. But to aid your understanding further, I wanted to share a few foundational terms we'll be using throughout the book.

Missional Leader
Someone who *mobilizes* God's people to join his redemptive work in the world.

Huddle
A discipleship vehicle for *leaders* that provides support, challenge, training, and accountability, and that is led by a discipling leader. Members eventually start Huddles of their own, creating a discipleship movement through multiplication.

Missional Frontier
Places or networks of people where there is little gospel presence and an opportunity for a much fuller in-breaking of the Kingdom of God.

Missional Community
A group of 20–50 people forming an extended family on mission together.

Oikos
The Greek word for "household," which refers to the 20–70 people, blood and non-blood, who made up the Greco-Roman household .

Character
Being like Jesus (the interior world of a person).

Competency
Doing the things Jesus could do (the external world of a person).

Disciple
- A person who learns to be like Jesus and learns to do what Jesus could do.
- Discipleship is the process of becoming who Jesus would be if he were you (Dallas Willard).
- Someone whose life and ministry reflect the life and ministry of Jesus.

UP/IN/OUT
As we see in the Gospels, Jesus had three great loves and thus three distinct dimensions to his life:

- UP: deep and connected relationship to his Father and attentiveness to the leading of the Holy Spirit.
- IN: constant investment in the relationships with those around him (disciples).

- OUT: entering into the brokenness of the world, looking for a response individually (people coming into a relationship with Jesus and his Father) and systemically (systems of injustice being transformed).

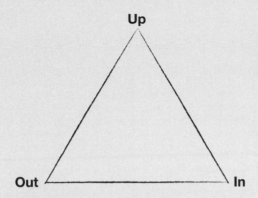

This three-dimensional pattern for living a balanced life is evident throughout scripture and needs to be expressed individually and in community life.

Kingdom Movements
A community that functions as a portal to the new world that God wants for all his children. A Kingdom movement is a community of disciples who passionately seek the expansion of God's reign here on earth through the reproduction of disciples, seeking the transformation of whatever places they inhabit.

Missional Sending Centers
Communities that have enough spiritual mass, with leaders who embody the character and competency of Jesus, to become places of reproducing, training and sending leaders into the missional frontier, as well as safe harbors of return and refreshment for these leaders whenever they leave a missional frontier, either temporarily or permanently.

✧ INTRODUCTION ✧

This is a book about movements.

But not just any kind of movements. *Kingdom movements.*

However, I need to say from the outset that this is not the first word, last word, best word, or only word on this topic. I do not claim to be an expert on movements. At best, as I have tried to understand what I've experienced, I find myself operating as an amateur anthropologist and sociologist.

I believe I can offer something that will give several perspectives that can help in the revelation of what we are discussing. And while I believe mine is an absolutely true perspective, *it is not a full perspective*. What I can offer to you are snapshots, not instant prescriptions.

Think about it this way: The scriptures give us pictures of God such as King, Shepherd, Warrior, Father, Adonai, Lord, etc. These are all ways of understanding who God is as we seek to be in a relationship with him.

There are many, many other characteristics and they are all true.[1]

---

[1] For those interested in diving into this kind of thinking academically, the person who helped me understand this on a deeper level was a brilliant man named Ian Ramsey, who is most famous for his journal article, "The Systematic Elusiveness of I." The part of his work that connected with me the most was what he called *models and qualifiers*, which had to do with the Philosophy of Religion. His basic premise was this: Throughout the scriptures, we get various descriptions of God. Each description gives another angle on the whole, and at some point we get enough of them to have a *moment of apprehension*.

At some point, something clicks, and we understand (at least in our finite way of understanding) who God is. It isn't that we have or understand all the perspectives, but we have enough of them. It is not a full perspective, but it is one that is absolutely true.

That is what I have to offer you.

I can give you various perspectives on the landscape of Kingdom movements, and I believe these perspectives to be true, but they are not the totality.

Let's use the metaphor of the Indian guide. As the Wild West of America was being settled, pioneers would pay Indian guides to get them from Point A to Point B. These guides knew the path that would get them to their destination, but it wasn't the only path. A guide doesn't know all the paths, just the ones he has traveled before.

Can the Indian guide traverse the landscape using the particular coordinates he knows? YES.

Does he know every hill, stream, mountain, and path? NO.

The Indian guide will tell you that the journey is perilous but possible. That's how I've written this book. There are mountains, lakes, rivers, farms, overgrown paths, and tales of journeys past that I know like the back of my hand, because it is the landscape of my life. I have had the privilege of being part of a Kingdom movement for the better part of my adult life. This book is my attempt at sharing some of the things I've learned along the way.

But it isn't the only way to get there.

In many respects, this is the story of what my life has been about for the past 40 years: getting caught up in a movement of the Kingdom that is changing the world.

So here's how I'd like to go about this. I want to share with you the story of the last 40 years of my life and what I've seen God unfolding in this world that he so loved. In the midst of that, I'll pull out practical, reproducible things I've learned along the way. You'll quickly notice that much of my story is learning from the mistakes we've made along the way. So in that vein, let me say this: **You'll make mistakes. But make different ones from the ones we've made!** That's one reason for sharing my story.

Another reason for sharing this story is to help illuminate Part 3 of the book, which is looking to the life of Paul as a guide for how to be part of a Kingdom movement. I've spent the whole of my adult life studying the life of Paul; namely, how did he accomplish so much in just one lifetime? I think beginning with my own story will help draw out, in a present-day scenario, what we see happening with Paul on a much larger scale.

Finally, throughout the book you'll see me going back, over and over again, to what is necessary for any Kingdom leader: the journey that must happen within. It is not an easy journey or one that usually ends with fame and accolades, but it is the journey every person must take if they want to change the world.

PART 1

∽ THE AGE OF ∽ EARTHQUAKES

Where we are:

In Part 1, I want to identify where we are. What is the reality in which we find ourselves? Perhaps the best way to shape the future is first to understand where we currently stand.

Where we are going:

I want to lay the foundation for a new, yet old, way of being the people of God. Namely, that *movements* have always best characterized the way of the Kingdom.

1

∾ IN THE RUBBLE OF ∾ THE EARTHQUAKE

(Some of you have chosen not to read the Introduction to this book. You really should read it. This book will be a much better read for you if you do. Now...on to Chapter 1.)

I've never met someone who doesn't want to change the world.

Never.

There is something wired deep within us that longs for the gap between the way the world is and the way it should be to be just a little narrower after our time here on earth.

People want to change their street. Their city. Their country. The world. It's always been buried deep inside us, but now we are seeing it more and more in the language of our culture because of this innate longing.

Everyone resonates with wanting to change the world. The problem is, they also say, "I have no idea how to do it." There is a great, yawning divide between what we want to do in our lives and what we end up accomplishing with our lives. So here's my question, the one I've been asking for as long as I can remember: What are the markers of the people who want to change the world and then actually go and do it?

Now let me be clear. I don't mean they amassed some sort of impressive personal empire, be it spiritual or otherwise. *I mean they legitimately changed the world.*

I remember hearing Jo Saxton (whom we will talk about later on in the book) talk about something that deeply impacted her when she was 12 years old. Jo is from England, and she was in an English history class. Her secular textbook pointed out that because of John Wesley and the early Methodists, two important things occurred. First, the civil wars that ravaged the rest of Europe at the time never touched the shores of the U.K. Second, the abolition of slavery could be directly connected to the influence of the Methodists within English society. Right there, in her school textbook, John Wesley was credited with helping to change the world.

And like everyone else, I'm interested in changing the world. I believe there is a God-given longing to reverse the curse of the Fall.

So I'm interested in the markers of the people who did change the world. I've spent my life studying this and have been amazed how so many people end up going back to the life of Paul over and over again. So like the world changers of old, we too will look at Paul.

But first, let's set the stage.

SHAKING EVERYTHING

A little time ago, I went to New Zealand on a mission trip with my son. We made our way to Napier, where we walked around the streets with one of the pastors of the city. I pointed out to the pastor that most of the buildings had the year 1932 carved into the foundational stones and asked if that was the year the town was started.

"No," the pastor said. "The city started a long time before that. But in 1931, on February 3 at 10:47 in the morning, an earthquake measuring 7.8 on the Richter scale struck. And it destroyed everything."

"What do you mean *everything*?" I asked.

"I mean everything. Everything was ruined. Every building fell, and as they fell, the gas mains ruptured, and a terrible inferno consumed the whole city. Believe it or not, many, many people actually survived. But more amazingly, those hills you see over there to the northwest—that was a plain. Those hills weren't there. And you see that mountain that juts out into the Pacific? Half of it just fell into the sea."

"Do you know where my home is?" The pastor continued. "That was the harbor for the fishing fleet. The harbor disappeared in a moment and became dry land."

It's hard to believe, but he was telling us that you couldn't even recognize the geography after the earthquake.

We have seen appalling, Hiroshima-like images appearing on our TV screens from natural disasters (or man-made devastations) such as Haiti or Chile or Japan. We have seen what lives are like when people build their homes on seismically active fault lines. We have seen the difference in responses between a poor and corrupt country like Haiti and a relatively developed and put-together country like Chile or Japan. We have seen it.

But no matter what the preparation was, or what the follow-up is, these tragic events remind us that sometimes everything is shaken.

Don't be surprised. **This is the age of earthquakes.**

IN THE SHADOWS OF A GREAT SHAKING

I always am able to best locate grounding points by starting in the scriptures. So let's begin there.

Hebrews 12:26 – 13:8

At that time his voice shook the earth, but now he has promised,

*"Once more I will shake not only the earth but also the heavens."
The words "once more" indicate the removing of what can be
shaken—that is, created things—so that what cannot be shaken
may remain.*

> *Therefore, since we are receiving a kingdom that cannot be
> shaken, let us be thankful, and so worship God acceptably
> with reverence and awe, for our "God is a consuming fire."
> Keep on loving one another as brothers and sisters. Do not
> forget to show hospitality to strangers, for by so doing some
> people have shown hospitality to angels without knowing
> it. Continue to remember those in prison as if you were
> together with them in prison, and those who are mistreated
> as if you yourselves were suffering.*

> *Marriage should be honored by all, and the marriage bed
> kept pure, for God will judge the adulterer and all the
> sexually immoral. Keep your lives free from the love of
> money and be content with what you have, because God
> has said,*
> > *"Never will I leave you;
> > never will I forsake you."*

> *So we say with confidence,*
> > *"The Lord is my helper; I will not be afraid.
> > What can mere mortals do to me?"*

> *Remember your leaders, who spoke the word of God to
> you. Consider the outcome of their way of life and imitate
> their faith. Jesus Christ is the same yesterday and today
> and forever.*

The writer of the book of Hebrews is unknown. Perhaps this is coming from
the Apostle Paul, awaiting his own death in Rome, hearing of the Jewish
rebellion and offering wisdom for the future to those living in his homeland.

The readers and hearers who first poured over this text were Hebrew believers
in Jesus, who were scattered across the four corners of the known world. It

seems written particularly to the Jewish Christians in Israel. Before this text was written, the Jews had risen up against Rome, and the emperor was fed up with the insufferable insurrectionists located in Israel. So the emperor dispatched his best general and the might of the Roman military machine to crush the zealot rebellion.

Let's be very clear on this: slaughter and complete destruction were on the way. The Jewish people had seen it before and knew what was coming. Foreseeing this, Jesus seems to say in some of his closing conversations with his disciples, "When the eagles are circling over the city, GET OUT."[2] He was probably talking about the Golden Eagle sitting atop the legion's standard as the Roman army approached.

Jesus, in his youth, had seen the retribution of Rome. Right around the time of Jesus' birth, a rebellion arose in the city of Sepphoris, about four miles from Jesus' hometown of Nazareth, and the Romans were called in to put it down. A Roman column stormed through Sepphoris and the city was destroyed and the population was enslaved. Houses were torn down brick-by-brick, and whole neighborhoods of the city were burned to the ground. Jesus' father Joseph, a carpenter by trade,[3] was probably one of the workers who helped rebuild the city in the decade that followed. Jesus may well have learned his father's trade rebuilding the devastation caused by the Roman army.

Now, at the time the Book of Hebrews was being written, the Jews living in Judea and Galilee were about to experience the reality of Roman destruction at a much greater level. Soon the walls of Jerusalem would be broken. The holy city would be sacked. The Temple and its treasures would be stolen or destroyed, never again to be used in worship by the Jewish people. The rebels would make their last stand at Masada and by the end of April of 73 AD, it was all over.

We are right on the precipice of this as the writer speaks about the world shaking.

There was a push within Israel for the Jewish Christians to come back to their roots, to join the rebellion, to leave the sect of Christianity. They were being

....

[2] Matthew 24:16-28

[3] Probably better understood as a builder or stone mason

squeezed on every side. Their world was being turned upside down, and they were starting to buckle under the pressure.

It's interesting that the writer of Hebrews lists out, almost verbatim, what emergency workers are taught to do when they triage a disaster situation.

- **Step 1.** You need to have *compassion* for the victims of the tragedy and get them the care they need as quickly as possible.

- **Step 2.** Once they've made it out of the other side, you re-connect people to *community*. Often times in disaster areas you'll see huge tent cities of refugees.

- **Step 3.** Help people grapple with the loss they've undergone and *connect them to a bigger story* so they can move forward.

- **Step 4.** Give them some firm, stable next steps (a *compass*, if you will) for re-creating a life that will need to find a new normal.

What the writer was saying is this: The world in which you find yourself is in upheaval. There is seismic change. You need to prepare for that seismic change. And as you do so, you need to attend to some basic things. That's because in a world of shaking and change, you can become self-centered and self-absorbed. But you are to keep the **COMPASSION**[4] of God burning in your hearts.

Remember to love, to stand alongside and to embrace those in greater need. Remember that in your tendency toward self-preservation, you will self-centeredly look to meet your own desires and needs. You need to keep yourself pure and to keep your own raging desires at bay. You need to turn away from self-interest and turn toward the **COMMUNITY**[5] you are a part of. Build the community. When everything else is being broken, you need to tend to community. The writer of Hebrews is saying that in times of pressure, we tend to isolate ourselves and we need to fight that impulse.

Remember that as everything is shaken to its elemental parts, as the world and society are atomized and separated, there is a **CONNECTING STORY**[6]

....

[4] Hebrews 13:1-2

[5] Hebrews 13:2-3

[6] Hebrews 13:5-6. *Connecting Story*: Sociologists call this a metanarrative. We use both terms.

that connects you to all of the people of God down through the ages, that connects you to all of the Christians who love the Lord, and that connects you to those who gave you entrance to your faith.

Remember your story.

Then, in the midst of all of this disorientation, in the midst of upheaval and social transformation that can best be described as chaos, remember that you can find your way because there is a **COMPASS**[7] that is the same yesterday, today, and forever. No matter how disoriented everyone else is, you can still be oriented toward true north.

We are the people of God. *Remember who you are.*

THE AGE OF EARTHQUAKES

We all know that earthquakes are not confined to the physical realm. We are in the midst of social and cultural upheaval. Social commentators, philosophers, cultural observers often use the language drawn from the world of earthquakes—talking about *seismic change*. If we've watched the news recently, we've probably heard this term.

Our world is changing. The fault lines obscured below our culture and our communities are revealed as hidden powers move.

Since 9/11, no one can argue that the earthquakes have reached the shores of the United States. As the Twin Towers fell, we all knew that the world had changed. And we all knew that the world had changed again when, seven years later, the twin towers of Banking and Finance crumbled in a slow-motion collapse that we all watched with growing horror.

If we still doubt that we are in the midst of shaking, then perhaps we need to look a bit more closely at what is happening around us. In fact, the world has been in upheaval for quite a while. It's just that this upheaval didn't reach American shores until recently.

....

[7] Hebrews 13:8

LIQUEFACTION

In seismically active zones, such as the Jordan Rift Valley, there is a geological phenomenon that almost boggles the mind. It's called *liquefaction*. When a layer of more fluid strata (layer of earth) lies below a nearly stable strata, the fluid strata begins to move and rise during an earthquake, and sediments stop acting like a solid and begin acting like a *liquid*.

In other words, in certain times of upheaval, things can be shaken so violently that even the properties of the earth seem to change. Solid becomes liquid. Such events give rise to shocking images when buildings and other objects move and even sink in the fluid earth!

As a result, buildings that were built on a strong foundation suddenly are anything but stable. It's fascinating to see the pictures. These buildings will remain completely intact but now sit at a 45- or 90-degree angle, unable to fulfill the purpose for which they were built.

The church finds itself in such a position today. Even churches that were built on strong foundations find the ground beneath them turning into liquid. We have no idea what to do about it. I mean, how do you build a church when you don't even know if the ground it is sitting on is going to remain a solid?

I believe the answer is in building *Kingdom movements*. The answer is in building something that has a strong foundation but is also infinitely flexible. There are grounded, fixed points that in some ways might resemble an organization, but upon a closer look actually reveal the nimble and flexible nature of the organism.

What earthquakes can also do is show us if we are flexible enough. Earthquakes help us respond. I may even dare say that from time to time, the church needs a good earthquake. Why? *Because in the wake of cultural earthquakes, the church has often been at its most effective.*

Let's pause here for a moment, because it's really important for us to understand the nature of the earthquake we find ourselves in.

Around the turn of the 19th into the 20th century, in Paris, the great artists and philosophers of the day—Jean-Paul Sartre, Simon de Beauvoir, Pablo Picasso, and even Ernest Hemingway—gathered on the *Rive Gauche*, the left bank of the River Seine.

There, they cultivated a culture that had been emerging in Paris for quite some time after the French Revolution. They used that newfound freedom to develop a philosophy that influenced so many of the thinkers in that culture. On the *Rive Gauche*, they explored a different world. They imagined a world that existed separately from the anchor points of the past. This world, in their minds, was liberated from the thinking of old.

"What would it be like if we understood morality from the point of view of the individual?" Sartre asked.

Simon de Beauvoir argued, "Surely we should liberate women from the servitude they have been subjected to for so long."

The *Rive Gauche* cultivated and promulgated these ideas. Before long, like a wind blowing on a dandelion head, these thinkers scattered their thoughts and ideas.

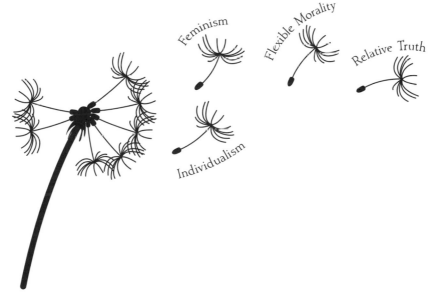

These ideas first gravitated to the wealthy of Europe and England in particular, who, because of their wealth, funded salons and academies throughout Europe, including the universities of my native nation, Oxford and Cambridge. There the thinking spread and grew. With the dawning of a new century, in these great centers of learning Europe began to feel an earthquake that shook every strata of society. As the old structures crumbled, these new concepts were released to spread further.

At the close of the Second World War, and the rise of a more mobile and more educated population, these artists and thinkers continued to gain acceptance in these centers of education. The growing world of *mass media* soon allowed these ideas to become more mainstream.

Baz Luhrmann's brilliant film *Moulin Rouge* is an interesting movie that depicts this happening. In it, we see this Parisian life come alive and Paris becoming the epicenter of a new world. It's fascinating, however, that the music of the movie isn't from that time, but from ours. We see how this Bohemian culture produced the soundtrack of our lives; that this culture discussed the things we now all believe. The flash cards that come up during the movie drive this home:

TRUTH.

BEAUTY.

LOVE.

And although the following lyrics are not part of the movie's soundtrack, songs we know so well illustrate the philosophy of the Left Bank:

Imagine there's no heaven. It's easy if you try. No hell below us. Above us only sky.[8]

Perhaps another: *All you need is love. All you need is love. All you need is love. Love. Love is all you need.*[9]

....

[8] From John Lennon's song "Imagine"
[9] From The Beatles' song "All You Need is Love"

Some of the most famous popular songs in recent history came from the philosophy of the *Rive Gauche* more than 150 years ago.

SHAKING AMERICA

Our world has been in the midst of seismic change for quite some time. But it hadn't really reached the shores of America until the 1960s began. Amazing things happened as the world strained and stretched, as old ways of thinking were broken. In some ways, that was good. In other ways it was anything but.

On the good side, we have the emergence of great movements led by illustrious leaders. Dr. Martin Luther King, Jr. was one positive example. But at the same time, an upheaval, particularly in the youth culture, led to Haight-Ashbury and the psychedelic revolution. It was all happening at the same time. The epicenter was in Paris rippling to Monterey, Woodstock, and beyond. But the earthquake has rumbled on. Its intensity has increased. Its power to change has multiplied. And the magnitude of this earthquake demands that we attend to it.

If an earthquake occurred in your city tomorrow and left devastation everywhere, what would you do? Would you assume you were the victim or the rescue team?

We are the people of God. *Remember who you are.*

What would we do if we were the rescue team? What would we do if we were the only hope? What would we do if, even though we've been shaken, our lives had not been completely destroyed because where we stand is far more secure than where others stand?

Refugees need a place of safety. Victims of the earthquake need a place where they can run. As they run, it feels like a refugee camp. The megachurches of North America are, in many ways, refugee camps. Our societal upheaval has paralleled the growth of megachurches. These giant churches are often a feeding program to keep people alive.

We don't need to pick on them.

I don't believe for a second that running a feeding program is at all what pastors of megachurches want to do. Instead of aiming easy criticism, perhaps we should ask, "What would happen if the people of God became a movement again?" Just imagine what would happen if the megachurches became movements changing their cities.

In the early 1990's at St. Tom's, we rebuilt community through something now called missional communities (originally we called them "Clusters"). As we followed our "compass", Jesus led us back to the city core. As we embraced our community story, we decided to embrace a much bigger story and came to function as the rescue team. And do you know what happened? Eventually that simply became the identity of the people. That's how they understood themselves.

Put megachurches aside. What would happen if even a small percentage of all the churches of Western culture started to mobilize themselves as a movement of the Kingdom? What if churches in the midst of this disorientation and upheaval saw their primary responsibility as being the rescue team?

What if, in the shaking, the thing that was revealed was that our foundation was unshakeable? The writer of Hebrews said that all things are being shaken so that what is unshakeable will be revealed. Surely those who have been the most untouched by the earthquake have the greatest responsibility to care for those found in desperate and dire circumstances.

Surely they would be the rescue team because there was no one else.

And so we are.

COMPASSION

So what does the rescue team do? Well, we do the same things that emergency workers would do in the midst of a disaster area.

We go and survey the destruction, observe the state of things, and triage the circumstances. But with all of this our first response is COMPASSION.

Why are people so disoriented?

Because they are in the midst of an earthquake! Do you judge them for that, or do you have compassion for them? Do you alienate them because they are shaken, or do you reach out to them? There is an upsurge in sexual disorientation in our time—do we judge, or do we have compassion?

We must answer this question, because the devastation is all around us. We could decide to do one of two things. We could look around us, gather those like us, and build a ghetto because we have "secure" footings. Or we can decide that we've been enlisted as the rescue team.

I don't know what compassion looks like in your context. Where is the Spirit prompting you, as the rescue team, to show compassion in your context to the victims of the earthquake? What is it? Where is the compassion of Christ?

In the late 1980s, Sally and I moved to serve in Arkansas. And believe it or not, it was really fun being in Arkansas. We were there when the Razorbacks won the NCAA basketball tournament. We were there when Bill Clinton won the presidency. We were right in the middle of history, and then we moved to Sheffield, England, which is decidedly not in the middle of history!

Sheffield is in the north of England and it quite similar to the city of Pittsburgh in the United States. There, we did similar things to what we had learned in the other places we had served. Let's just say that in Sheffield, going to church was one of the least popular things to do. Maybe about 2 to 3 percent of people attended church at the time. We were in a deeply depressed city. The steel industry had collapsed, lots of people had left the city to find jobs, and unemployment constantly hovered around 12 percent.

We were in one of the suburban areas (not a wealthy area), and like Rome, our city was built on seven hills. The church of St. Thomas Crookes, perched on one of those hills, overlooked the city.

Every day, after I walked to my parish church, this old stone building, I gathered my team to pray. Sometimes we'd gather in the clock tower in the church, where you could see the whole city, and we'd just ask, "God, what should we do?" And the Lord said, "Just start building community here, and I'll tell you what to do next."

All the time, God was building our concern for the city. We had been out on the streets, we gave away stuff, we had kindness initiatives, we shared with people who were hungry, and we wrapped people's Christmas presents for free. We found anything we could do to connect, just to be out there.

And then the Lord said, "I want you to call the city back to me." We looked at the city and thought, "How can we call the city back to God? We live on the rim of the city. We'll have to move into the city."

COMMUNITY

Here's the thing about earthquakes: When all the buildings are destroyed, no one wants to go in them anymore.

No one.

They don't feel safe. When people have seen all the institutions fall to the ground, they no longer feel safe entering them. Marriage. Economics. Family. Religion. Politics. These institutions, being far too rigid, have collapsed, one by one, in the last hundred years. People feel the inflexibility of institutions, and out of a gut, instinctual reaction, they say to themselves, *"These 'places' just can't be trusted."*

If you were in the earthquake and you continued to feel the aftershocks, would you feel inclined to go into a building you thought might crash on your head at any moment?

During times of upheaval, we need community. And these times force us to think afresh about what it means to build flexible, portable communities. The reality of our time is that "the Church" does not feel like a safe and secure place for victims to go. People look at this fallen institution and think, *"This thing might fall on my head, and I don't want to get crushed."*

People still need a place to gather, a place for family, a place to call home, a place to find identity and meaning. However, they need places that feel safe and secure, away from the shaking and insecurity associated with the earthquake. And most are actually looking for faith. They hunger for something to believe in.

CONNECTING STORY

When an earthquake happens, everything that people base their life on is destroyed. Homes. Jobs. Families. In other words, *what most people base their understanding of identity and self on is completely removed.*

Most of all, they have lost their story.

There is a story that is bigger than us, and in that story, we make sense of our life and existence. The word often used is *metanarrative*. Because of the metanarrative, the connecting story, we know our place and how to function with meaning. But for most people, in times of brokenness and tragedy, the story is interrupted and perhaps even destroyed. It has all crumbled away. Devastation ensues, and the story of ourselves all but disappears.

When the screaming (in the midst of the earthquake) stops, the processing begins. How do you live with the cries in the rubble that you cannot do anything about? How will you live with the degree of brokenness that is in your life? Your metanarrative, the story you found yourself in, has been utterly shredded. Your identity was defined by your community, your culture, your story, but now it is forever changed. Where do you find your identity now?

People need a connecting story that is defined not by loss but by redemption.

We need to connect them to a greater story, a redemptive story that reaches into their world and into the rubble. The story of God and his people stretches through the ages, and we are part of it. As we embrace it, the story is continued and extended through us. Where once there was calamity, people now find the connecting story of redemption. We are now part of the rescue team. And so our life has immeasurable value and meaning.

COMPASS

In times of disorientation, the default mechanism we need to learn is finding our compass bearing again. But where do we go when the maps don't work anymore? It has all changed.

Metaphorically, I was given a whole bunch of maps at theological college as I was trained to be a vicar in the Church of England. The training was intended to teach me how to lead the people of God. One day, soon after I was ordained, I got these maps out again, blew the dust off, and suddenly realized that they bore no resemblance to the world in which I lived. *I was trained for a world that no longer existed.*

So the best I could do was to find a compass for myself and for my family—one that I could put it into the hands of everyday, ordinary people. What I found was called *discipleship*. Follow Jesus. And then teach others how to follow Jesus. He's the compass we can all follow.

Follow him. That is the message we carry.

Victor Hugo, in his immeasurably great book *Les Misérables* (which became the musical that everyone knows), had a fascinating insight. Reflecting on the upheaval of the French student riots in Paris, picking up on the metaphor of a ship adrift in the ocean, he says, "The ocean seeks to lead it astray in the alarming sameness of its billows, but the vessel has its soul, its compass, which counsels it and always shows it the north. In the blackest nights, its lanterns supply the place of the stars."

If we don't have maps, we have to have a compass.

As disciples of Jesus, we are the compass carriers. We carry, in ourselves, in the words of scripture and in the Body of Christ the spirit of Jesus himself, the compass that points north. "The Spirit that raised Christ Jesus from the dead is now alive in you."[10]

And that compass is the same yesterday, today and forever.[11] It will always guide you to true north. At the end of the day, after all of this is done and all fades away, it's about Jesus.

....

[10] Romans 8:11
[11] Hebrews 13:8

THE GREAT MOVEMENT LEADER

It's worth noting that there seem to be seasons where the world doesn't just need to change, but is actually longing for it. It's aching for it, desperate for it. That's how the world was in Jesus' time. And I believe we find ourselves in that world today.

We're not just talking about movements for any old time, but especially for the times where there is rubble lying around. In times when earthquakes have struck with such devastation, that it seems as if the only recovery is a sovereign God releasing a movement of his people.

History is a funny thing. It constantly repeats itself.

Leading up to one of the greatest movements in history was a time of unbelievable uncertainty and upheaval. The movement that would come out of it? The Reformation. What people a lot smarter than me will tell you is that everything that was present for the opportunity for the movemental change of the Reformation has happened again. Everything present for the sweeping change of the early church is present again. We are on the precipice of a new Reformation.

The question is, are we up for it?

Sometimes in these bigger moments, we point to one person or figurehead at the root of it; but really, it's the amalgam of many people and many things colliding together.

Think of the fall of the Berlin Wall.

When we think of the fall of the wall, we usually remember Ronald Reagan: "General Secretary Gorbachev, if you seek peace, if you seek prosperity for the Soviet Union and Eastern Europe, if you seek liberalization: Come here to this gate. Mr. Gorbachev, open this gate. Mr. Gorbachev, tear down this wall."[12]

---

[12] Excerpted from Reagan's famous speech, delivered June 12, 1987, set against the backdrop of Berlin's Brandenburg Gate, delivering a challenge to Soviet leader Mikhail Gorbachev.

Yet this was just one moment in time. We can't ignore all that came before it. There were decades of work, strategy and opportunity. The crisis moment of Chernobyl played a role. And we can't forget that the wall did not fall for a few more years when Reagan was no longer in office.

But here is where I think the rubber meets the road if we are seeking a movement of the Kingdom of God. In one place, where the wall still stands today, it reads: "Many small people doing many small things in many small places can change the face of the world." Long before the wall came down, a reformation was rumbling around in the hearts of people, forcing them to do many small things in many small places over and over again.

There is such a restlessness in the people of God today. They sense there is a drift, they sense a threat, and they long to be connected to a Christian faith that understands itself as part of something bigger, something movemental, something of the Kingdom.

This book isn't about one movement, but a series of movements that form a larger whole that is the Kingdom of God. It is about lots of people in lots of places doing lots of things and chasing after where God is already at work.

And this is nothing short of what Jesus was after.

What we see in Jesus is the ultimate movement leader. He was someone who, in three years, unleashed a movement that would change the course of human history. What we see in the early church, and specifically in the person of Paul, are people who did something very simple that has profound meaning for us today. **They simply did what Jesus taught them to do.**

In his parting words, Jesus said this: "Go and make disciples of all nations, teaching them to obey everything I have taught you."[13] That obedience piece is pretty important, isn't it? It reminds me of a G.K. Chesterton quote: "Christianity has not been tried and found wanting. It has been found difficult and not tried."[14]

What I want to suggest to you is this: Jesus taught his disciples how to lead

....

[13] Matthew 28:19-20

[14] From Chesterton's (1910) book *What's Wrong with the World*.

a movement that would change the world. And it worked. As we think about movements, we must begin with Jesus because he was the most gifted movement leader who ever existed.

I have spilled much ink in a few other books on how Jesus was able to release a certain kind of discipling movement that always leads to Kingdom mission.[15] So for the purposes of this book, I want to show how, when people take the teachings of Jesus to heart, they too can learn to be part of a Kingdom movement. As you will see, one way we will explore this is in the life of Paul.

It is difficult to imagine someone who took the "and obey everything I have taught you" more seriously than Paul. If Jesus said it, Paul took him at his word. For sure, Paul was an extraordinary man, but his capacity to lead a movement didn't happen overnight. The Lord shaped Paul for a task, over years of time, and formed him into the movement leader we see in the New Testament. On the road to Damascus, Jesus arrested Paul in a pool of light and with a booming voice. That was his compass-turning experience. Paul suddenly had a new normal.

The Lord is looking to do the same in us.

As I mentioned in the Introduction, I will use the backdrop of some of my story to help us explore the life of Paul. Then we will get to Paul. For so long, the story of Paul has been embedded deep within me, so it is a labor of love to share some of the things I've found in his life.

But before we get to Paul or my story or a discussion of Kingdom movements, it might help to return to the 'times' we are in and to use them to define what I mean by *Kingdom movement*. There are many ways to define a movement, but I think it would be helpful for us to consider several vantage points.

DEFINITIONS

As the team I serve with and I have considered this idea of Kingdom movements, we have come to some defining realities that we believe are central. Again,

....

[15] Most notably, in the books *Building a Discipling Culture* and *Multiplying Missional Leaders*

these are not THE defining realities or the ONLY defining realities; they are simply the ones we have experienced. We'd like to use these as a grounding point and explain them further as the book progresses.

Ultimately, a Kingdom movement is a community that functions as a portal to the new world that God wants for all his children. Put another way, a Kingdom movement is a community of disciples who passionately seek the expansion of God's reign here on earth through the reproduction of disciples, seeking the transformation of the places they inhabit.

ULTIMATELY, you've got a movement on your hands when the Kingdom DNA of something is so transformative and so reproducible that the Kingdom of God continues to expand with little-to-no direct effort from the "center." In other words, it takes on a life of its own.

- Kingdom movements are focused on making disciples of Jesus who can make disciples who can make disciples
- Kingdom movements are scalable and sustainable
- Kingdom movements are highly reproducible on every level of group size
- Kingdom movements are lightweight and low maintenance
- Kingdom movements are about low control and high accountability
- Kingdom movements have strong and flexible leadership patterns
- Kingdom movements often find identity expressed through axioms and icons
- Kingdom movements live on the continuum of *organized* and *organic*. These are not separate compartments that force us to live in an either/or reality but a sliding scale of the same reality

CONCLUSION

There can be little doubt that we live in a world of earthquakes, in a world of seismic change. We live in a world where even the substance beneath our feet can seem to change properties on any given day. However, in the midst of it all, we are reminded that the future often lies in the past. And with the history of the people of God, we find a deep and rich past that uncovers our own future. Movements not only survive but also thrive in times of upheaval.

Why? Because Jesus Christ, our great movement leader, is the same yesterday, today, and forever. And as he calls us to himself to learn from him, we say with one voice:

"We are the people of God. *Remember who you are.*"

PART 2
∽ MY STORY ∽

Where we've been:
We've identified where we find ourselves as the
people of God. I have laid out the vision for one of
the principal forces the Holy Spirit has used in
times of seismic upheaval throughout history to
change the world: Kingdom movements.

Where we are going:
In Part 2, we will look at my story and how these
ideas have played out in my life. In addition, at
key points in the story, I will make sure to stop to
examine a few of the things I've learned along the
journey.

2

❧ THE BREAKING ❧

The first book I ever read was the Bible. I was 16. It's not that I wasn't intelligent enough to read, but I had lived with dyslexia for all of my life, which made it nearly impossible to read. Somewhere between 15 or 16, the Lord rewired my brain, and suddenly I was able to read—and I picked up the Bible.

YOU'LL NOTICE **that in Part 2 I capitalize and bold certain words. This is purposeful as I will explore those same words in the life of Paul in Part 3.**

I wasn't a Christian. I hadn't grown up in a Christian home. But that was my first book.

The first Christian girl I ever met was a spritely young lady named Sally. I thought to myself, "If this is what Christianity about, I'm definitely in." We have been friends ever since, so to speak—she's now my wife!

We lived in England, and *post-Christian* doesn't begin to describe the religious carnage that has left this society in tatters. It is post-modern, post-Christian, post-... well, we could probably follow those descriptions with another 20 "post-somethings."

Maybe four to five percent of the population is in church.[16]

They are a group of people who have never really heard the gospel.

---

[16] A report from September 2012 now finds attendance at six percent and attributes much of this increase to the mid-sized, missional communities that you will soon read about.

I felt pretty quickly that God was calling me into full-time employed ministry, and so I entered theological college at 18. Now the natural decision for someone who was from my family background was to join the Church of England. It's a very broad church, so it has everything from the most conservative Christians all the way to the most liberal.

The college suggested I be ordained, very soon after my 21st birthday. I thought that was a bit young—since I had started shaving only the year before! I thought it might look a little silly, me being a boy among men. So I went into the inner city as a youth worker for a few years. While I was there, I did some research for a degree as a Student of Theology, which was given by the Archbishop of Canterbury. I then completed my post-graduate work at Durham University.

After a few false starts regarding where I was going to serve first in the church as an assistant,[17] I ended up in Cambridge (and not the university part of it but the town side of it, where many of the shift workers were).

For about two years, I lived in utter desperation. I had learned an awful lot during my training, but had gained very little. In all, my training took seven years, and I had three theological degrees, but I really knew less about how to engage with the Lord and do his work than I did before I entered theological college. The situation truly was desperate.

I can clearly remember an old lady saying to me, in a rather pietistic fashion, that she was praying that, at some point, God would give me *some kind of fruit* to demonstrate that I was called to ministry! She was trying to be encouraging, but it really came across as a double-edged sword. Obviously, she also was wondering if I had been "called" to this work. (For her, the jury was still out.)

I used to practice and prepare and do the best I could on Sundays and visit people in the hospital and try new things—I did everything I could think of, everything I knew how to do. And absolutely nothing worked. NOTHING. A growing feeling of failure and a looming sense of catastrophe were just over the horizon.

....

[17] It's called a Curate in the Church of England.

It felt like I was trying to push water up a hill with a rake.

One day I was clearing the backyard because our firstborn, Beccy, had started walking. I decided we needed to clear the undergrowth that was quickly consuming the yard. The grass was getting so long that you could almost hear the noises of the jungle. Who knew what kind of wild animals might be hiding in the tall grasses?

So I got a double-handed scythe (perhaps you've seen one in old photos) and began to drive back the wilderness and chop down all of the grass. As I did this, I came across two nests of red ants. We don't have many biting ants in England, but these definitely were. I could see visions of my toddling little girl being overrun by carnivorous insects. I thought to myself, "I really ought to kill these things."

I looked at them but just couldn't think how to kill them. One at a time was certainly too time-consuming. My mind was absolutely blank. Then I thought, "I wonder what my dad would do in a situation like this?" The answer probably reveals my limited gene pool. When I asked him later what he would have done, he said exactly what I thought was the solution: gasoline. In England, we call it petrol.

I went into the shed and got the gas can. Now Sally (my wife) was taking a walk with Beccy, so there was no one around. It was the middle of August and a sunny day (a rarity there). I splashed the gasoline around on the two anthills. Apparently, this would have been enough to kill them. After all, ants don't prosper too well while drowning in petroleum. But I wasn't done—I went to find some matches.

For the life of me, I couldn't find them. Sometimes I wonder if God had placed an angel in the house, desperately trying to hide the matches to keep me from perpetrating the foolishness that was about to ensue.

Finally, I found some matches on top of the cabinets, and I went out into the yard and struck a match. I discovered you didn't even need to throw it because immediately everything was burning. The whole yard. Flames were leaping everywhere. I stepped back in horror (the poor ants had their own private Hiroshima), and I saw a trail of fire all the way back to the gas can. I looked at that and thought, "You know, that's really not good."

I needed to get that can away from those flames, and quickly. So I grabbed the can, which of course was hot. Now if you want to make a flame-thrower, you get a can of gas with a spout, and you light the spout, and then you eject the contents of the can through that spout. I know because that's exactly what I did when I dropped the burning hot can. Now there were gouts of flames leaping from the can all over the backyard and onto me. My feet and my trousers were on fire. Everything slowed down at this moment. I had NO IDEA what to do.

All I could think about were those BBC public information films that we used to watch at school: "In the event of a household fire, stop, drop, and roll around on the ground."

Well, I couldn't exactly do that.

The ground was all on fire!

"Get a blanket," the public service announcer would say next. There was no blanket! The only thing I could do was take my trousers off. Now I had been trained in the Church of England, and running about the yard without any trousers was not what a good English clergyman was supposed to do. I had a brief moment of hesitation, but I had no other options. I flipped off my running shoes (which were also burning), and *of course* one of them went over the fence into my neighbor's yard.

Now *his* grass was on fire.

And just as I was about to take my trousers off, completely at the end of myself and with nothing left, I shouted at the top of my lungs, "Lord, HELP ME!"

In an instant, everything stopped. As I looked down, I saw that not only were the flames on me extinguished—they were also out in the yard, which was fantastic. I went back into the kitchen and did the thing that all Englishmen do in a crisis: I made a cup of tea. The kettle was almost boiling when my wife got home and said, "What's that smell? There is this terrible burning smell." I told her the story.

"Let me see your legs," she said.

"They're fine."

"Show me."

I complied, and as I took my trousers off, I looked down and to my horror saw large folds of skin on the bottom of my legs just kind of hanging there. I looked at Sally and said, "That doesn't even hurt." She was ashen at this stage, and she ran and called a taxi so that we could rush to the emergency room. As I got to the ER, the pain hit. Up until that point, my body had been in complete shock.

Over the next three days, the third-degree burns got infected and became septic. In the operating room, they scraped off all the burnt stuff, and took a huge piece of skin from my thigh. They put that piece of skin into a fridge until the burnt areas were ready to take it. Then I was put in isolation.

They left me at a 45-degree angle, all alone, not able to see Sally or Beccy or anyone. Every once in a while, they would get to wave to me through a small glass window. Once a day a nurse came in and, as far as I could tell, tortured me. She had to remove the bandages to see if I was still bleeding. "Is there no way to find out without taking the bandages off?" I asked in what I'm sure was a completely polite tone. It was just unbelievable pain.

I lay there, day after day. This hospital was one of those more British, stiff upper lip institutions where they didn't think that television promoted healing. No television. Someone smuggled in a tape recorder (yes, I'm that old) with the testimony of John Wimber on a tape. As I lay there, feeling so stupid and desperate, I kept asking, "Is this really what it's going to be like? Is this what I'm destined to do for the rest of my life? Frustration? Failure? Nothing happening. I am so stuck. Is this it?"

And in that quiet stillness I heard the Lord say, "Let me do it."

Let...me...do...it.

That moment, everything changed for me. I slowly started to realize that Jesus is much better at the work of discipleship and life than I was or ever would be. He had given me some gifts and some abilities and skills, but I had absolutely no idea how to use them—not in a way that could produce the transformation of which the Gospels spoke.

It may sound silly or simple or strange, but almost everything that I want to share with you is how to learn to let God do the work that he is already doing. He is already at work in your life. He is already at work in the life of your family, your community. He is already breaking in and breaking through.

I started to notice something very odd. The more time I spent listening to God, and the more time I spent asking him to show me where he was already at work, the more spiritual breakthrough I saw in my life and in the life of our community. The closer I was to God, the more breakthrough I saw. It was absolutely amazing. By simply paying more attention to where God's Kingdom was already breaking in, and by resting in him, I spent far less energy and produced far more fruit.

It was like one of those things we hear Jesus say in parables but never quite get because it's so counterintuitive: in God's Kingdom we get more of a return than what we originally invested. We invest two and get four back. We invest five and see a return of 100!

That had never been my experience before this point. My experience was that it was always like pushing a boulder up a hill. My experience was that I had to crawl, scrap, and scrape for every inch of spiritual breakthrough I'd ever seen.

But this period of breaking in my life was a linchpin for everything that was to come.

Psalm 102:23-28 really helps me understand what was going on in this part of my life.

> ***In the course of my life the Lord broke my strength;***
> ***he cut short my days.***
> *So I said:*
> *"Do not take me away, my God, in the midst of my days;*
> *your years go on through all generations.*
> *In the beginning you laid the foundations of the earth,*
> *and the heavens are the work of your hands.*
> *They will perish, but you remain;*
> *they will all wear out like a garment.*

Like clothing you will change them
and they will be discarded.
But you remain the same,
and your years will never end.
The children of your servants will live in your presence;
their descendants will be established before you."

BROKEN TO LEAD

What is certain is that God uses all the circumstances of our lives for our benefit—even the circumstances that lead to our breaking. It's important for us to understand that there is a deep and significant role of breaking in our lives.

As I survey the pages of scripture and look over the vast majority of Kingdom movements in the last 2,000 years, I see one striking reality: at the center of each movement were leaders who had been completely and utterly broken in such a way that they came to rely completely on the Lord for everything.

Peter. Paul. James the Just. Augustine. Patrick of Ireland. Jackie Pulinger. Aidan. Abbess Hilda of Whitby. Mother Teresa. Luther. Wesley. The list goes on and on.

You see, people are not born movement leaders. My observation is that the people who go on to help lead Kingdom movements are those who have been willing to embrace an unbelievably difficult breaking experience in which God was able to form something deep within them by constantly returning them to this truth: "Remember, my power is made perfect in your weakness."

In this breaking, we come to the utter bankruptcy of our capacity. We are unable, in our own strength, our own skill, our own competency, to do one more thing. We can't fix the situation. We can't solve the relational dynamics. We can't keep the community from disintegrating.

These situations occasionally come into our life, and we find ourselves so completely bereft of emotional, spiritual, and physical energy that we can barely stand up against these things, much less defeat them.

"In the course of my life, the Lord broke my strength."

What's the purpose of these things in our life? They help us discover a greater strength.

One of the things that we will naturally do because of the disposition of our fallenness is to look at ourselves as the solution to any problem. Since the Fall, each person has been looking toward himself or herself as the center of his or her own universe.

In the end, this really is a vain pursuit.

When we get to the point of incapacity or inability, either we give up (which is what often happens), or we give God the opportunity to do something in our lives. And sometimes, we actually need to do both.

This breaking is a pattern we see in scripture in the great heroes and heroines. It's certainly a pattern I see in my own life. I can't even count all the times I came to a place where I just didn't know the way forward. The only way that something could get fixed was if God stepped in, because obviously he is slightly more resourceful and powerful than I am! *But I had to choose to let him.*

From what I've discovered, this is my practical suggestion: learn to recognize the signs early.

Rather than coming to a place of complete spiritual, emotional, and physical exhaustion and utter dereliction, recognize the signs early that you are coming to the end of yourself.

The scriptural word for that is **humility**.

In other words, **you don't wait for everything to be broken to recognize that everything is broken. Rather, you continually step into a posture where you realize that, if left up to you, you'll break everything anyway.**

We need to get to the point where we surrender our desire to fix everything and our sense that we are the solution to our lives. We've all been in situations where we've had the opportunity to learn that, but letting that lesson graft into our heart is something else altogether.

In the Chinese church, one of the great saints of the 20th century was a man named Watchman Nee. He told a story that gets to the heart of what we are talking about. One of his disciples said to him, "Do we have to be continually broken over and over again so we learn this lesson?"

With his characteristic wisdom, he simply said, "No."

"Well, how then does it work?" his disciple asked.

Nee asked the disciple to hand him one of the shortbread cookies on the plate next to them (we'd call it a biscuit in England). The disciple picked up the cookie and handed it to his teacher.

"Often," Nee said, "we feel like this cookie," as he held it up in front of him. Then he broke the cookie, which is not difficult for an adult to do with something so fragile.

"That's what you feel like when you're broken. You lose your sense of togetherness. You lose your sense of inner integrity. You lose your sense of anything that makes you feel like you have any coherent identity."

Then he put the cookie back together in the palm of his hand. "Can you see where it is broken?" he asked.

"No, I can't," the disciple said.

Of course, you know that when you put a shortbread cookie back together, it fits together perfectly. You can't even see the little hairline fracture in it.

"Look at this," Nee said. "All I have to do is touch the cookie with the *lightest* of touches, and you'll see that crack again. Here's the thing: Once you've embraced true brokenness, you don't have to experience it again and again. All God has to do is lightly touch you, and it reveals the tiny crack. That's the key."

That's what is revealed in Psalm 102. The psalmist had been brought to this place of brokenness, and he felt as if his days had been cut short. But immediately, the brokenness forced him to look at the capacity of God. The psalmist's inability helped him look at the ability of God. The psalmist's temporary life allowed him to view an eternal life. He was able to hold them in balance. He realized that an eternal perspective is not found in his own brokenness but in the strength and completeness of God.

The ultimate reality lies in God.

As the psalmist did all that, his life turned from hopeless to hopeful.

Paul remarked about what it's like to bear in oneself the suffering and affliction of Jesus—about what it is like to come to the end of oneself and truly recognize that if the Kingdom is going to advance, it'll be God doing it and not us. This is the realization that in my own strength I actually don't have anything to offer.

At the end of the day, you aren't smart enough, gifted enough, charismatic enough, relational enough, strategic enough, disciplined enough, or loving enough to release a Kingdom movement. You simply don't have it within you.

And that is a good thing.

Because when I am weak, he is strong. 2 Corinthians 12:9 (and the verses around it) became my life verse during this period.[18]

I imagine you have already had great breaking experiences in your life. The question is not necessarily whether you've had them but what you did with them. Did those experiences do something in you in such a way that all the Lord must do is tap the cookie of your life and the hairline fracture of brokenness appears? Is there a posture of humility? Or is there still a fundamental belief that you've got it within you to do this thing?

....

[18] 2 Corinthians 12:9-10: "But he said to me, 'My grace is sufficient for you, for my power is made perfect in weakness.' Therefore, I will boast all the more gladly about my weaknesses, so that Christ's power may rest on me. That is why, for Christ's sake, I delight in weaknesses, in insults, in hardships, in persecutions, in difficulties. For when I am weak, then I am strong."

3

∾ THE SPIRIT ∾

$oon after the events that led to my breaking, Sally and I were called to one of the poorest communities in England, a part of London called Brixton Hill. One day I felt the Lord say to me,

"I want you to carry the cross around the streets of Brixton."

"Yes, Lord! I can do that. What a brilliant metaphor. So what do you want me to do?"

I heard nothing else.

So, I went away on a retreat to pray and listen to God on it. I was waiting for him to tell me what I was supposed to do. But all I got was this recurring picture of me carrying the cross around Brixton. That was all I got.

I thought, *"I really get that. Pick up the cross. Follow you. Yes. That's what I want my time here to be about."*

I remember sitting on some rocks overlooking the Forest of Dean on that retreat when the Lord gave me this scripture passage from Hosea 10:12: *"It's time to break up your unplowed ground and seek the Lord until he showers righteousness on you."*

Wait.

Oh no.

"You mean it... you mean it... literally, don't you? You literally want me to carry a cross around Brixton Hill! Brixton Hill—one of the most dangerous places in Britain?"

I laugh about it now, but at that moment, I almost had a sense that some angel who had been assigned to me during that retreat loudly exhaled and said, *"Whew. He's FINALLY got it. I can leave now."*

So I went back home and talked it over with Sally, more than half-hoping that she was going to talk me out of it. *"Sally, I've been listening to the Lord, and I think this is what he's asking me to do..."*

Pause.

More pausing.

"Yeah. Yeah, that sounds about right to me."

Great. Just great.

So I started constructing this giant cross. Our neighbors were twitching at the curtains, wondering what in the dickens I was up to. I walked around the church parking lot with this giant cross. It was a small parking lot (not a lot of cars could fit), and I was just circling around it, thinking, *"Why in the world did I make this thing so heavy?"*

I told my team at the church, *"Look, this is what God is saying to me. I'm not trying to put it on you. I'd love to have you join me, but you certainly don't have to."*

"Great. We won't be coming then."

I said it to the congregation and invited them as well. They looked at me like I was absolutely mad. The first day, it was just me. No one else was with me. When I stepped out on the road, it was like walking into one of those saloons in a Western movie where the pianist stops playing. Everything just came to a standstill. I got to the corner of the street, and I was physically shaking.

I gathered my wits and yelled at the top of my voice, *"Jesus says he is the light of the world!"*

I looked up to see a third-story window open, and I heard someone say, *"Blimey, the vicar's gone mad!"*

I preached a couple of more minutes and then dragged the cross down the street. I passed a coffee shop, and I saw my youth pastor inside. He looked at me and silently mouthed the words, *"I'm praying for you."*

Thanks very much.

But a few days later, he joined me.

A little while after that, a few more joined me. What I had to learn was how to deliver the message of Jesus. This was a society that was lost and broken, and they would never hear the gospel unless someone did something slightly crazy and out of left field.

Now this probably isn't appropriate for where you live. To be honest, I wouldn't have done it aside from the Lord telling me to do so. But it proved to be a place of breakthrough for the community as people gathered to the cross to hear the gospel. People came to Christ, right there on the streets. People were healed of all kinds of ailments and sicknesses.

It was at this place in my life where the idea of connecting the **MESSAGE** of Jesus with the context of people's lives really began to take root. It wasn't that I had fully learned it, but it began the learning process in me. **It instilled in me the idea that nothing was off the table for how God might want to communicate his message of love.**

And out of that breaking, God began to do things in me and through me. We began to see the miraculous happen all around us.

MIRACULOUS

One day we were out on the streets of Brixton Hill, and I met this woman named Irene. We got to chatting a little, and she said,

"I've heard about you. You're the vicar who carries around that cross, aren't you?" (It wasn't a great insight on her part, as I was carrying the cross at the time!)

"Yeah. That's me. Is there anything we can do for you?"

"I don't think so, I'm fine. Thanks."

"Anything we can be praying for?"

"Well, actually... I did twist my ankle this morning, and it hurts quite a lot."

"OK. We can pray for it."

She nodded and started to walk away.

"Wait. Why don't we just pray for it together right now?"

"Here?"

"Yeah. What we'll do is keep our eyes open like we are having a conversation and invite Jesus into the conversation. That'll be the prayer."

"Oh, well that's clever."

So I put my hand on Irene's shoulder and began to pray. *"Lord, I just pray for Irene... "*

... and she exclaimed, *"Ooh!"*

I continued, *"and heal her... "*

"... Oh!"

"Jesus, we ask that your Kingdom would come, that your Holy Spirit would make Irene's ankle whole again."

"Whoah! Blimey vicar, he's done it! My ankle is healed!" Then suddenly she turned, ran up the road, and disappeared around the corner.

I looked at the people with me and asked, *"Does anyone know where she lives?"*

"Uhhh.... no."

"Well, that's a good one! We need that one."

The next day a few of them came to me and said, *"We think we know where she lives. We think she's at 93 Commonwealth Gardens."*

"How do you know that?"

"We asked the Lord."

Well, honestly. What do you do in that situation? Sure, I've got faith that says the Lord could deliver that kind of revelation, but honestly, even I'm not sure I'm seeing this happen. But not wanting to discourage this group, I said, *"Well, he'd know, wouldn't he? Let's go see if that's it."*

We went out, and what we found is a gap between the row houses. This particular address had been bombed during the war and had never been rebuilt. Clearly, she wasn't living there.

The next day they came back to me and said, *"It's not 93 Commonwealth Gardens. It's 39. We got it wrong."*

"So you're telling me that God is dyslexic like me?"

Again, I was their pastor. I wanted to be encouraging. It just seemed to be utterly ridiculous. But I went out with them to 39 Commonwealth Gardens. I knocked on the door, and Irene opened it. *"Hello, vicar. Good to see you again. What are you doing here?"*

My jaw hit the floor.

"You know those people who were with me when I prayed for you when your ankle was healed? They were praying for you and felt like God gave them your address because there was more he wants to give you. So here we are."
"Well, he'd know, wouldn't he?" She invited us in for a cup of tea, and she became a disciple of Jesus right then and there.

The **MIRACULOUS** is hugely important in seeing the movement of God.

One of the most important things that Sally and I learned early on, though, was that if it was going to be a movement, the miraculous had to be done by the people with the people and not simply by the clergy.

So we began to train the congregation how to live a life that embraced the supernatural, but in a natural, non-weird way. **My observation is that most people reject the gift because of the package. So what if the packaging wasn't weird?** And what if we had a theology for when people aren't healed?[19]

We trained people on what it would be like to embrace the supernatural in each of the four spaces. What does it look like to pray for people, Christian or

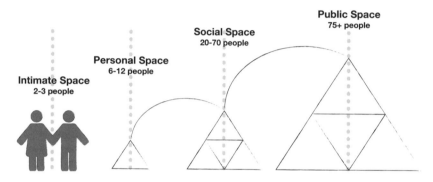

Intimate Space
2-3 people

Personal Space
6-12 people

Social Space
20-70 people

Public Space
75+ people

IDENTITY FOUND HERE

not, in groups of two or three (intimate space)? What about personal space (groups of six to 12)? What about the Missional Community setting (groups of 20–50)? What about public space (the worship service)? As we created space for them to practice, succeed, and fail, they began to embrace a life in which they believed the Holy Spirit was constantly at work, and they were discovering how they could join him.

Here's what people often forget: things like Missional Communities are a fantastic vehicle for mission. They really are. But without the embracing of the Holy Spirit, it's just another thing you're doing on your own. We have seen MCs and other missional vehicles multiply at exponential rates and have seen people come to faith in huge numbers not simply because the methodology is solid, but because the Holy Spirit is at the center of it all. It's his power in the simple, ordinary things of a supernatural life that is making all the difference.

....

[19] That will be another book for another time.

To use an analogy I've used before: if Missional Communities are the vehicle and discipleship is the engine, the Holy Spirit is the fuel. If you don't embrace the Spirit of Jesus, I don't care what your methodology is, it's going nowhere. We are creatures of overreaction. We jump easily from ditch to ditch, and many of us have thrown the baby (the power of the Holy Spirit) out with the proverbial bathwater (a style of 'ministry' we might find repellant). Perhaps we need to learn to live with a different packaging rather than rejecting the gift wholesale.

The miraculous is not just for the specialist. It's for everybody.

A FAMILY OF SOLDIERS

In the midst of all of this, I came to understand something central to the gospel of Jesus. Ezekiel gives us a brilliant picture for this. He describes the people of God coming together as dry bones assembling in a valley, and suddenly it is a mighty collection of soldiers. Not one soldier, but a whole army.

It is true that in the Kingdom we are called to be soldiers. But we must remember we are also a covenantal community, which means we are a family. The picture Ezekiel gives us is of a *family of soldiers*.[20] There needs to be as much emphasis on the family as there is on the soldiers.

What I've noticed is that faith traditions tend to veer toward either the Covenant side (family) or the Kingdom side (soldiers). For those who lean on Covenant, life is about the JOURNEY that the Covenant community is making together. They live rich, full lives together, but often win very little ground for the Kingdom. On the other side, for those who lean more toward Kingdom, life is about the BATTLE that is being fought for the Kingdom. Often they gain ground for the Kingdom, but they can quickly lose that ground because there are so many family casualties along the way. That happens because they don't attend to the family aspect as well. In fact, they can sometimes sacrifice their family on the altar of ministry.

It has to be both Covenant and Kingdom.

....

[20] In Ezekiel chapter 37

Jesus is the Great Shepherd, but he's also the Warrior King.

It's a family of soldiers. It's about a family's journey through life together as they fight Kingdom battles along the way.[21] This was something that we saw over and over again in Brixton Hill. Sally and I always have this natural pull to Kingdom, to the battle. But we can't keep any ground that is won if it is done apart from a Covenant family.

There is a journey, and there is a battle.

There is a family, and there is a mission.

---

[21] John Bunyan's incredible book *The Pilgrim's Progress* is perhaps the best picture of this I've ever seen.

4

ꙩ GRACE AND FAITH ꙩ

··

As I've alluded, after we had spent a few years in Brixton Hill, God sent us to Arkansas for a little while before I took the job of Team Rector in Sheffield, England, at St. Thomas. We continued to tinker with the Missional Communities we had first stumbled upon in Brixton, but we still didn't fully understand what God was revealing to us.

In 1994, I took the post at St. Thomas. It was a church rich with a tradition of new missional expressions and a pioneering spirit. This church had started what Eddie Gibbs called the first alternative or "post-modern" (not in the theological sense) worship service.[22] It was called the **Nine O'clock Service**.

The Nine O'clock Service was a truly amazing environment. During the 1980s, it became quite the magnet for new missional approaches, as some of the best leaders in Europe and North America came to see what the Nine O'clock Service was doing and how they could learn. Unfortunately, as sometimes happens with wildly successful churches, the leader turned quite inward and became almost sociopathic, and, if that wasn't enough, deeply immoral. We don't need to get into all the gory details, but it was ugly.

This congregation (which by the time I came to St. Thomas was its own church) was closed by the Church of England shortly after the scandal erupted.

Those were the difficult circumstances surrounding my new ministry, and, to make it worse, the story seemed to run forever and ever in the media.

··

[22] For more information on this service, we'd recommend reading the Wiki article on it, as it gives a good summation of how it began, the influence it held, and where it ended up.

We were on television every day and on the front page of the newspaper all the time, because the only physical building that could be associated with the Nine O'clock Service was our building. Even though we were no longer officially connected, we got all the spotlight.

So clearly after that process, learning to cultivate a culture of accountability and discipleship was huge.

I had a sense of many of the things that I wanted to do going in, things that I had learned in the last 15 years that I'd want to implement. But before I could do that, we first needed to identify reality.

There is one helpful analytical tool I've picked up over the years to help me do that, and it's one with which many businesses and communities are familiar: the SWOT analysis. It is one that we continually refer to on our team to understand what is happening in our movement, where God is moving, what he might be up to, and how we might respond.

On one continuum, you have **strengths** and **weaknesses**. On the other continuum, you have **opportunities** and **threats**. When you put these two continuums together, you get a matrix that looks like this:

This creates four different quadrants. What we've learned to do is think about this through a spiritual lens. What happens, in a spiritual sense, when opportunity and strength meet in your community? Simple—Kingdom breakthrough. What happens with an opportunity for your community is met with a community weakness? Frustration. What happens when a weakness in your community is met by an outside threat? Failure. What happens when a strength in your community is met by an outside threat? Battle.

Breakthrough.
Frustration.
Failure.
Battle.

So at any given moment, you can identify all sorts of things happening in your community. Where is there Breakthrough? Frustration? Failure? Battle? It's not like the whole community is all in one quadrant. All communities and all movements are a mixed bag. We have things in every quadrant.

And we usually have one response for the quadrants marked by Frustration, Failure or Battle: work harder.

Of course you know by now that I think this response is wrong. Don't work harder. Remember, this is spiritual. Our battle is not against the temporal realities of this world but against something else. This is a spiritual reality, and so we need a spiritual solution.

ANSWERING BATTLES WITH GRACE

If you find something in your community in battle, what will move it from battle to breakthrough? You feel like you're hitting brick wall after brick wall, and it's happening in an area of strength! Some kind of force outside your community is keeping you from seeing a breakthrough. Maybe it's a zoning commission. Maybe it's hearts that are unusually hard and aren't responding to the gospel.

Maybe you have a team working in the inner city fighting all kinds of injustice, a team that has seen extraordinary breakthrough in the past, but it's just not happening this time. You should be winning. You should be bringing down the Kingdom of Darkness. But you find yourself in a huge Battle.

The answer? **Grace.**

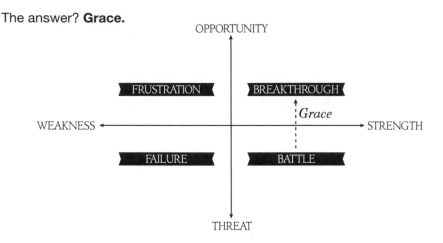

In Luke 11, the disciples were coming off a mission trip where they had seen some success but a lot of battle. Then Jesus started going after the religious leaders again. Here are a few from the highlight reel:

- "Clean the outside of the cup and dish, but inside you are full of greed and wickedness."
- "You neglect justice and the love of God."
- "You are like unmarked graves, which people walk over without knowing it."

You know, there are some slightly *offensive* things there.

The disciples had to be wondering, "Will this man ever just leave them alone?" They were fearful of what might happen if Jesus angered these leaders any more. After calibrating a dialogue about fear, Jesus, noticing how worn out, tired, and battle-weary they were, says, "Fear not little flock. Don't you know that my Father is pleased to give you the Kingdom?"[23]

....

[23] Luke 12:32

The Father's gift to you is Kingdom breakthrough. It's not yours; it's his. That's why Jesus so emphatically said in John 15:5, "Apart from me you can do nothing."

As you probably already know, the Greek word for grace is the word "gift." So in the midst of battle, how do we get to breakthrough? We look for the gift. We look for where the grace of God is already at work and mine that vein of gold from the place where it is at work.

Here's an example.

I can remember how difficult Sally and I found our time in Arizona when we first arrived in the U.S. after our time at St. Thomas came to an end. The grace of God was in just a very few relationships of people who loved us and were open to what we had to share. One such family was the Rapps—Kevin, Jo, Brontë, and Leighton. We had no idea when we first met them, but they would prove to be one of the stabilizing relational influences in our life for years to come. So when we left Arizona they came with us as part of our 'family on mission'—and they are still with us today! Their coming with us from the battle helped to bring a breakthrough as 3DM[24] was launched into its work from South Carolina, the United States, and now across the world.

We literally couldn't have done it without them. They were God's gift of grace to us at the time, one we couldn't possibly earn.

Find the grace. Always be looking for it. Look for where the Spirit is already fighting for you in this area, and join him there.

Don't work harder. The Spirit is already doing the heavy lifting for you.

ANSWERING FAILURES WITH FAITH

If you find something in your community that is marked by Frustration, what will move it to Breakthrough? This is a wall of a different kind. This is where you can see, as clear as day, the opportunity for your community. You can

....

[24] 3DM is the organization I currently lead. It trains Christian leaders on five continents how to do discipleship and mission in an increasingly post-Christian world. For more: *www.weare3dm. com*

taste the breakthrough. The Kingdom is unfolding before your very eyes, and *the frustration lies in the fact that your community has a weakness that perfectly coincides with your opportunity.*

Maybe there is an opportunity to purchase a building that will serve as a missional sending center for a whole region, but the people in your community have never been strong givers. It's the perfect building, but the money isn't there. Maybe there's a housing project that is ripe for the Kingdom to advance and for people to come to know Jesus and the chains of injustice to be loosed, but you don't have any missional leaders who know how to do cross-cultural ministry with a marginalized people group.

Whatever it is, you look at the situation and want to pull your hair out in frustration.

The answer? **Faith.**

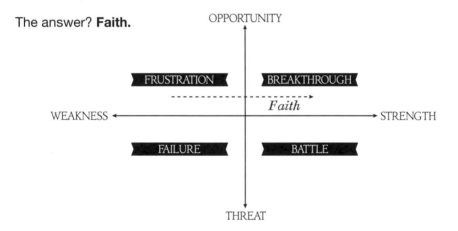

We know that disciple means "learner" in Greek. So what we need are people who believe that God is calling them to learn to do something they currently don't know how to do. How does this connect to faith? "Faith comes from hearing the word." **We need God to speak to our community in such a way that it sparks in them enough faith to take a step forward.**

"I've never been particularly good at giving, but I feel like God has spoken to our community and to me personally, and he is asking for me to give in a sacrificial way. God has said something to me, it has produced faith in me, and now I'm going to do something about it."

"I'm not going to lie. I really don't know much about working with a marginalized group of people, but God has made it very clear he's calling me to this. And I may not start out too well at this, but with time and God's spirit, I can learn. God has said something to me, it has produced faith in me, and now I'm going to do something about it."

Faith isn't just attached to that specific thing God is saying to us. We also remember all the things God has said in the past where he acted and was faithful. That builds in us a wellspring of confidence that the Lord will continue to be faithful.

This isn't blind hope.

God has a proven track record of being faithful. And so when he speaks something to me and I act, I know he will take me from frustration to breakthrough.

For example, when we first started 3DM, we didn't just need a few people to help us get the thing off the ground; we needed a great team. But we were specifically led by God to a community (Pawleys Island) that did not seem to have the people who would make up this kind of team. In fact, several friends and church leaders we knew thought our way of being a family on mission was really odd! How could we build a team in a retirement beach community in South Carolina?

At this point, frustration could have easily set in. But as we followed God's lead, our team found us. Everyone who joined us moved to be with us through pretty significant sacrifice. They stepped out *before* the financial support was there for them. God helped us grow a team without us having to spend money we didn't have. We moved to Pawleys Island and had faith God would be faithful (not blind hope), and he grew the team we needed to fulfill the calling.

When we find ourselves in Frustration, we need to create spaces where people can hear from the Lord and are given the opportunity to respond in faith. We don't just need a cleverly formed plan. We need to hear from God first and foremost.

But there is one last key to this.

It begins with you.

Living in faith and grace needs to be the warp and woof of your life. Leaders create culture. If you want a culture that looks for the grace in Battle and responds to Frustration with faith, you have to model that for them.

In your life as a leader right now, where is there a Battle? Where is there Frustration or Failure? Where is there Breakthrough? God is calling you to find the grace and respond with faith.

A THREE-DIMENSIONAL COMMUNITY

So let's jump back to the St. Thomas's story.

Clearly, as I walked into St. Thomas, battle, frustration, and failure abounded. But breakthrough was also happening. By looking through a lens like this, I was able to discern, with the help of the Holy Spirit, some of the ways we could move forward as a community.

Creating a discipling culture was incredibly important, so we needed to model everything we did after Jesus. I wanted to create a culture that had three dimensions to it just as Jesus did: UP/IN/OUT.

UP: deep and constantly connected relationship to his Father and attentiveness to the leading of the Holy Spirit.

IN: constant investment in the relationships with those around him (his disciples).

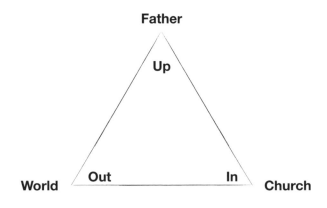

OUT: entering the brokenness of the world, looking for a response individually (people coming into relationship with him) and systemically (systems of injustice being challenged transformed). The result was God's Kingdom advancing.

We began to use UP/IN/OUT as our language.

It's interesting that once you start to use language of a particular kind (language that is simple, portable, and repeatable), it really does start to shape and form a culture.

Very quickly people started to ask questions like this: "Is your small group doing any OUT?"

Simply by giving people a lens and helping them understand that their lives and communities needed to have all three dimensions of Jesus' life, we started to develop a missional culture. We started to experiment more and more with small groups working together (maybe three to four small groups for a total of 40-50 people) on a common mission, and some things began to emerge. At the time, we called them *Clusters*, but over time, these mid-sized missional groups started to be called Missional Communities (MCs).

For us, this is how MCs were born at St. Tom's.

To launch the three-dimensional culture we told some of our small groups, "OK, this is what your monthly rhythm could be. First week do UP, second week do IN, third week do OUT, and the fourth week, why don't you get together with those other two or three small groups and do something together."

Eventually the people came back and said, "It's interesting, we like the small groups, but we *really* like that bigger, mid-sized group. We love that time together. We've even given it a name. Is that OK? And is it OK if we spend more time in the bigger group and do mission together?"

Ummm... yes. It was OK.

They were starting to identify more and more with a group about the size of an extended family and do mission together. The small groups became a place of support and accountability. Over time, we started putting more emphasis on starting these mid-sized groups and letting the small groups emerge *within* them rather than just clustering them together.

Clearly, this was a period of great transition in our church, and because of this, there needed to be large amounts of patience and grace. Fortunately, the Holy Spirit provided much of that, because for me it can sometimes be in short supply.

I remember one small group in particular I was working with.

"This OUT thing you keep talking about, we're not quite sure what to do."

"Well," I said, "you will probably need to leave the house."

"Wait. You don't want us to be like Jehovah's Witness people, do you?"

"No. I don't want you to be anything other than who you are. But the fact is that there are more people outside the building who don't know Jesus than there are people in here who do. So until we change that, we haven't finished our job."

"But we don't know how to do that."

"Well, what are you good at?"

They said they were good at UP and IN. "OK. Why don't we take what you are good at and use that? Why don't you go out into the neighborhood you feel called to and go pray for folks?"

"Do you mean actually walk up to them and pray for them?"

"No. Just walk around and prayer walk. Pray for the neighborhood, and pray for people in your head as they pass. Think of it as silent carol singing."

So the group went out and walked around their neighborhood, stood on street corners, and silently prayed for people. After a little while, they came back and said, "This is amazing! We got this sense of God's presence and power, and then people came up to us and asked what we were doing."

"What did you say?"

"We told them we were praying for the community, that God's Kingdom would come. As they were leaving, they told us things we could be praying about in their lives, and then they'd leave. What do you think we should do now?"

"OK," I said. "Why don't you do this? When you are standing there on the corner, have someone go and knock on a door, and when they answer, just tell them that this group is praying for the community and ask them if there is anything specific you can be praying for them about."

They tried it and came back. "You'll never guess what happened."

"Try me," I wryly remarked.

"Well, we went out. We asked people if they wanted prayer for things, and everybody was suggesting stuff to pray for. But then someone went too far. They totally broke the rules."

"What rules are those?"

"The ones we made up! We all agreed that we would just collect the requests and not pray for people on their doorsteps because it would be too embarrassing. And one person just decided to break all the rules, and they prayed for them right there on their doorstep… and they were healed right then!"

"That's fantastic! So you've taken something you're good at, combined it with something you're not good at, and it produced something you're better at. That's great."

Of course, some of these early Missional Communities were sterile and weren't able to give birth to new mid-sized groups, but a few became incredibly productive and multiplied several times over.

You certainly wouldn't say that it was a sweeping success or a home run right off the bat. But it was a start. And that's all you need most of the time. Just a little sliver of breakthrough that you can build on that builds faith for the things to come.

ACCOUNTABILITY

So we were seeing these MCs starting to develop—again, this is the very earliest stage of their history. The church was growing rapidly. At this early stage, we imported a very simple accountability maxim that we pulled from Matthew 18:15: ***Don't go and speak to any pastor about an issue that you have with another member of the congregation unless you have first spoken to that person at least twice. If you try, all we will do is turn you around and send you straight to them.***[25]

We had the same rule for the staff team because it had to be the same rule for everybody.

That Matthew 18:15 culture was hugely significant in the life of the church. It later became ingrained in the discipleship vehicle we developed called Huddles, which would prove critical a year or two down the road. I think it was the chief reason why, after I married more couples than I can count, there was not a single divorce in the 10 years that Sally and I were there.

Not one.

And to this day, some years later, I can really think of only three.

The environment that a Huddle creates is one where people are invited into relationship and challenged to be who God has called them to be, and so it creates this beautiful culture of accountability. Maybe you treat your spouse badly, but you're not going to go long before that relationship has to be mended because people are holding you accountable to what God is asking you to do. Sometimes people think of accountability like spiritual policing; when done well, it's actually spiritual partnership.

....

[25] Later, we will look at how to build a radical community so that a red-hot center will slowly develop. This Matthew 18:15 principle was *essential* in seeing a radical community begin to flourish in our community.

GROWING

That culture continued to roll on, and the building simply wasn't big enough. At this point in time, we had four services (two in the morning, two in the evening), and it was standing room only. We had this very real sense that God was giving us a specific mission: **call the city back to God.**

It wasn't just the suburbs where we were located, on the rim of the city—it was to be the whole city. And if that were to happen, we would need to have a presence in the city and the suburbs.

I went to the Bishop and asked if he could give us a few other buildings in the city that were no longer being used. There was a precedent for this—another church, Holy Trinity Brompton in London, had been given additional buildings. But the Bishop said this:

"Never. Watch my lips so we are very clear. *Never.*"

"Well, here's the thing, Bishop. I have no room left in the church. What am I supposed to do with all of these people?"

"Why do you want to grow any more?"

"Because it's the gospel imperative, and it's what Jesus wants us to do. Go and make disciples and such. If disciples go and make disciples... you kind of end up with more people..."

And I kid you not, he said, "Yeah, I don't think that's right. You're putting too much pressure on the other clergy, so I need you to stop growing."

"But I'm not really even doing anything. It really Is God!"

"That's great, but I need you to stop it."

Needless to say, there was a certain 'separating of paths' at that point.

I went back to my team, spent some time with them, and soon came back to them with a plan. We would take somewhere between two-thirds and three-quarters of the church and re-plant it into the center of the city, which had been devoid of a vibrant Christian presence for years. It wasn't just the normal "white flight" of the Christian Church that we see in Western countries, but the dismembering and dismantling of the church that we have seen happening all across Europe over the last couple of generations. This pattern meant that cities like Sheffield had, at best, a few tiny congregations, and the enormous, ornate buildings were simply edifices of an era gone by with no one in them.

Statistically, Sheffield had just under 2 percent of the population in a church each Sunday. A *good-sized church* had about 39 people (seriously).

So when I say it was a post-Christian context, I really mean it.

I turned up at the meeting that was set up to discuss this further, and the Bishop was waiting there with the assistant Bishop, both Archdeacons, and the Dean of the Cathedral. The Dean was there because I was planning on moving into his parish (the parish is a geographical area for which a church was responsible).

In other words, I was encroaching on his territory.

I said to them, "Here's what we'd like to do. We'd like to take the majority of our congregation and go downtown where there really isn't anyone and go worship in the huge gym by the Cathedral." To say that they weren't exactly pleased would be a bit of an understatement.

Somehow, miraculously, I got them to agree to an "experimental period" where we'd try this out. (Of course, in my mind experimental would last something like 50-100 years!)

So we moved down into the heart of the city. We met in this gym, or really more of a large sports facility, and it was absolutely awful. It had all of the echoes of a huge bucket, and people were constantly walking in and out on their way to play football[26] or work out. It was a terrible place to meet, but there was nowhere else to go.

On top of that, at the end of the first year we needed to increase our budget

....

[26] Call it soccer if you must.

by 50 percent, overnight, to stay there because the cost of leasing it was so exorbitant. I told the congregation this, and on a single Sunday, the whole community covenanted to give the 50 percent increase that was needed. And they did.

Then, literally the next day, the largest nightclub in the north of England went bankrupt, and the building was offered to us. It's called the Roxy. It was where the Rolling Stones played before they got really big. It was just a massive space, which in other eras would have been called a pagan temple, and we got it. And along the lines of the Celts of old, we just painted it and moved in. It's not like our enemy is going to hang around. If you want to get rid of the darkness, just turn the light on. So we did.

We put new carpet in.

We attempted to clean the toilets.

The toilets were probably the largest in the whole of Europe. I'd never seen anything like it! You could probably get 10,000 people to go at the same time if you really wanted to.

The carpet that we laid (and this is part of the St. Thomas folklore now) didn't even need adhesive to stick down. It just laid right on top of the carpet that was already there, because when you stepped on the original carpet, it made this popping or sucking sound when you tried to pull your foot away because it was so sticky from all of the old beer, gum, and other junk on it. It was just gross.

We put the carpet on it (and it too stuck).

Painted.

And started worshiping.

RELATIONSHIPS AND RESOURCES

When we got the Roxy, something very important was happening. In the years to come, we would lose this building and be homeless for a year. Although we thrived in that year we were homeless, we could *sense* it just wasn't sustainable. We needed a center of training for gathered worship, training, and mission. A place we could gather. A place from which we could resource the movement that was starting to emerge.

In many of the books and articles I've written, I've focused more on the relational and spontaneous nature needed for discipleship and mission to happen if we want to see a Kingdom movement. The reason for that is because so much time and attention have already been spent on the resourcing and structure needed for any organization to work.

But I want to make sure I am clear and say that we need *both* working together well.

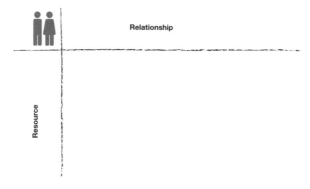

For any sort of relationship to multiply well in a sustainable way, it needs to be resourced by something greater than itself. I fundamentally believe this.

As a practical example, let's say you are leading a church or a youth group or a non-profit, and you are intentionally investing in six Missional Community leaders. All of them are leading groups of 20–50 in different cracks and crevices of your city, seeing the gospel incarnated in those places.

Here's a real-life example. One of the leaders on my team in Pawleys Island planted a church. Here were a few of the Missional Communities in that community:

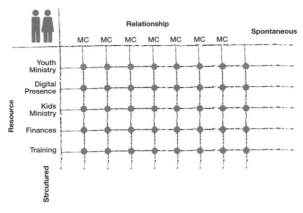

- MC for artists

- MC for the homeless

- MC for people in a particular marketing agency

- MC for young families

- MC for people who had adopted kids
  (20 different nationalities represented!)

- MC for a particular wealthy neighborhood

While it's fantastic that you are investing in them relationally and spiritually, you also want to see them get the resources they need so they can be as effective as possible.

So each Missional Community isn't expected to function completely on its own, but is getting the necessary resources it needs in a structured way so it can do what it does best: function in relationships with people in a more organic, spontaneous way.

This is the tension in which movements need to live.

If we are going to be talking about movements that have resources, they are going to need resources!

Hopefully you've noticed that whenever I have a question about something, my first inclination is to turn to the scriptures. And it's no different here. How do we fund a Kingdom movement?

I've found that the early church gives us a very simple picture that helps us understand this: Give. Share. Make.

GIVE

Surely we are familiar with the idea of giving, particularly in modern evangelical churches. Almost exclusively, the needs of the community (whether it's buildings, salaries, overhead costs, mission trip funding, communal needs, funds for loosing the chains of injustice, etc.) come from the funds that people give out of their tithes and offerings.

To be sure, we should continue to disciple people to give generously and help them choose to give rhythmically and regularly. But this isn't enough, for two reasons. First, this kind of economic model is only one way we see Jesus and the early church operating (we'll get to Share and Make in a second).

But second, it just isn't sustainable right now.

In the average Western church today, a disproportionate amount of the budget for a church is provided by the giving of those more than 65 years old. The statistics would astonish you. In comparison, the giving of Gen X, Gen Y, and even the younger Boomers is quite low, with each successive generation giving less and less. Without coming across as crass, what happens when the older generation passes on?

On the current trajectory, the future of the church is bankruptcy.

Let me give one anecdote to highlight this point. A few years ago, a well-known pastor stepped down from the pulpit of his megachurch and handed it over to someone else. In very short order, a large contingency of the congregation left the church, and giving plummeted. In just a few short months, this church was teetering on the edge of economic disaster. The former pastor had to come back in order to save the ship. Who were the vast majority of people who left? The older generation who gave a statistically disproportionate amount of the budget.

Should we be discipling people to give generously from the other generations? Absolutely. But as I've written before, we are in the midst of a discipleship crisis in the Western church, and there will be a gap, even if we attend to that problem.

My guess is that this will soon become a reality for many churches if we operate with an economic model only based on Give.

SHARE

Many of us are so familiar with the famous passages from Acts 2 that familiarity has bred unfamiliarity. Let's look again: "All the believers were together and had everything in common. They sold property and possessions to give to anyone who had need."

We often miss the context in which this was happening. On the day of Pentecost, the church went from 120 people to 3,120 in one day. A few verses later, Luke indicated that it was growing each and every day. The apostles, probably with divine wisdom from the Holy Spirit, decided to try to keep the church in Jerusalem for these formative years. After all, what does church even mean? It had never existed until this point. They needed time to get their feet underneath them.

Pentecost is one of the festivals where Jews who were scattered in the Diaspora would return to the holy city. Jerusalem's population would swell from maybe 60,000 to several hundred thousand for a few weeks and then return to its normal population.

Suddenly, thousands of people who usually would leave were now staying. Barnabas was a good example. He wasn't from Jerusalem; he was from Cyprus but stayed in Jerusalem. Furthermore, history suggests that by the time of the stoning of Stephen, eight years into the life of the church, there might have been as many as 20,000 people in the church in Jerusalem, many of whom weren't from Jerusalem. The population of the city would have grown by 20 to 30 percent in only eight years.

What escapes us are the economic realities of this situation.

The economic landscape of an ancient city wasn't meant to change that quickly. It would buckle underneath the pressure. There weren't enough jobs in an urban center for this kind of influx—not to mention houses for them to stay in. A city of 60,000 couldn't instantly grow to 75,000–80,000 and stay within the city walls. There simply wasn't space.

So all of these early Christians were constantly looking for work because there weren't enough jobs to go around. They were always looking for a place to stay because there wasn't enough housing. But the apostles knew that if they scattered too early, it wouldn't last. They needed time.

So they committed to being a radical community.

People who had land, farms, businesses, or homes in other places of the world sold them and brought the money to the apostles, and everyone's needs were met. People shared what they had, whether it was food, medicine, or housing. It didn't matter. This wasn't communism. This was survival for a community that wouldn't survive without them sharing. It just wouldn't work.

In this picture we understand quite clearly the best way to understand the church: as a spiritual family on mission together. That is what we see in the early church. It was a family that was radically committed to each other in all aspects of life. If someone had a problem, they all had a problem.

Intuitively, I think we get this. We know that if our parents or grandparents, siblings, or children found themselves destitute, we'd share what we have in such a way that they could survive. Why? Because that's what families do.

I would argue that because the Western church has embraced a model of church that is Sunday-centric, one that revolves around the large gathering of the public space worship service, we have lost this essential capacity to be family and care for one another in this way. You can't be family like this with groups of hundreds or thousands of people. Because of that, we have become more and more atomized into our nuclear families (the small group size), where everyone is fending for themselves. Where spiritually, emotionally, and often economically, it can feel like a fight for survival.

In a Kingdom movement, though, we move to places of communal identity that once again re-locate themselves in the *oikos*, the extended family of 20–50 people. In this social space, when there is a need, it isn't faceless or removed from our relational reality.

By embracing the *oikos* again, we embrace an economic model of sharing where the needs of the family are my needs as well.[27]

....

[27] We will spend much more time examining *oikos*, families on mission, etc., in Part 4 of this book.

MAKE

This is the principle with which we are most unfamiliar.

Usually when we associate "Make" with the church, we think of bivocational pastors. The church is struggling, or the church is just starting, or the pastor isn't really good enough to merit full-time pay, so he or she has to get another job and do ministry on the side.

First, I think there is a pretty unhealthy stigma that attaches itself to being bivocational, strangely enough, even with church planters. This seems to be the train of thought:

- A "real" pastor does ministry full time for full-time pay
- If you're good enough pastor, you'll be paid full-time.
- If a pastor isn't paid full-time, it's because he or she isn't good at his or her job.
- Most people find their identity in their job (an unfortunate reality).
- If I'm not paid full-time, it means I'm not a good pastor.
- Therefore, the core of my identity is shaken because I'm bivocational.

That's the stigma.

I want to suggest that movement leaders won't buy into this. They simply won't care where their salary is coming from. I am currently leading a team that, if you were to add it all together, would be the size of a church. In the biblical and ecclesiological sense, it pretty much functions like one. But that's not where I'm drawing my salary from, and I couldn't care less.

Paul started a Kingdom movement that changed the course of Western history and did it in his spare time. That didn't seem to bother him too much.

Movement leaders won't care if their salary is coming from a church or somewhere else. Why? Because of two words that I think define Kingdom movement leaders above and beyond leaders of Christian institutions: *disciplined* and *entrepreneurial*.

This isn't to say that there are not institutional leaders who are either disciplined or entrepreneurial. It's simply to say that when you put those two things together, you often get something that looks different from an institution. It tends to look more movemental.

People who are disciplined and entrepreneurial aren't the type of people who feel the need to draw an institutional paycheck. They believe in the idea of movement so deeply within themselves that their identity won't be shaken because of the lack of an institutional paycheck. Maybe it comes from there; maybe it doesn't. But, by and large, these people are already thinking of inventive and creative ways to fund movements outside the box.

So there's the whole bivocational reality. If I were a betting man? I'd put my money on the idea that in 20 years we will see a massive increase in the number of bivocational pastors simply out of organizational necessity.

That being said, bivocationality is only a piece of a much bigger pie.

What we really need are economic engines that can fund movements that come outside Give, Share, and bivocational Make.

In our long and illustrious past, we have seen whole missional movements funded by economic engines outside these fiscal realities—movements that evangelized whole continents.

Let's take the monastic movements of the 5th through 15th centuries as an example. These spiritual households, usually made up of 30–70 men or women, were largely responsible for the evangelization of Europe. If you dig into the history of it (I highly recommend this), it will change the way you think about movements, evangelism, funding, and family.[28] These spiritual families largely didn't receive funding either from parishioners or from the state.

How were they able to fund this missional operation? They had economic engines.

They had farms. Owned property. Threw fairs. Ran businesses. Were beekeepers (seriously). You name it, they did. And they didn't just do it—they made a lot of

....

[28] Two really good books on this are Joseph Finney's *Recovering the Past* and George Hunter III's *The Celtic Way of Evangelism*.

money doing it. How much, you may ask? Here's a peek inside history.

In the 16th century, when Henry VIII became king of England, he inherited a vast fortune from his father (to the tune of £375 million, in today's currency). Henry was always good at squandering money, and he quickly found himself on the brink of financial ruin. But he found a financial loophole that saved the country and his reign from being a complete disaster. (To be fair, it probably was a disaster regardless.) When Henry broke away from the Holy Roman Church, he passed an act called the Dissolution of the Monasteries that proved to be quite shrewd. In claiming all the property and holdings of the monasteries of England, he immediately put £36 million back into the royal treasury every single year.

Every year, that's how much the monasteries were making. Most were caring for the poor, and for hundreds of years, the monasteries had funded missional movements and adventures to tribes of people not living in the Kingdom of God. By and large, these were not communities that exploited marginalized people groups, but instead communities that sought the release of the marginalized from tyrannical injustice.

These people knew how to make money, but they also knew how to use it for the Kingdom.

That's what we need.

In fact, we have started an initiative called The TOM Project that is looking at starting a movement on college campuses across the United States and Europe. One of the primary focuses of this initiative is equipping each campus community with an economic engine that can lead to self-sustainability outside of denominational funding or personal support-raising.[29]

We need to create economic engines that will release Kingdom movements. We need economic engines that are not good at making money simply for the sake of making money, but good at making money for the sake of releasing successive generations of movements.

Where are the movement leaders who will take us to this new (and old) reality?

....

[29] For more info, you can visit *www.tomproject.org*.

5

❧ THE MULTIPLICATION ❧
YEARS

St. Tom's finally had a place to call home, a missional sending center. All around us, we saw battle, frustration, and failure. But having built a discipling culture over years, we were seeing untold amounts of breakthrough as well.

The local TV station came out and just started interviewing people. All they would do was put a microphone in front of people and ask,

"Why are you here?"

"Well, I was in prison, I was a drug addict, and one of these people visited me and I became a Christian."

"Why are you here?"

"I used to be a prostitute and they met me on the streets and I came to know Jesus."

"Why are you here?"

It was the best advertising anyone could ever have. Every night, in prime time, we were covered on TV. We didn't have a marketing budget—all we had was our lives. The church grew by 500 people in a few short weeks simply because they saw us on TV. They came looking for transformation.

So now, we had thousands in our church in a place where 2 percent of people went to church and the average church size was 39.

It was a giant.

Along the way, I can remember one day above others so very clearly. God asked me, *"Do you want to be a megachurch pastor, or do you want to be this other thing?"*

Other thing? What other thing?

"God, what other thing?"

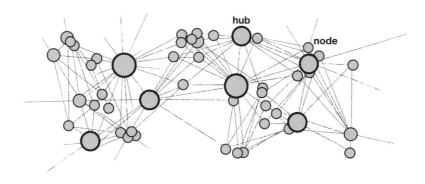

He gave me this vision of—it's hard to describe—this network of communities that kept extending and going and going and multiplying and was led by the people, not the pastors. It was a picture of a movement. It was no longer growth by addition, but growth by multiplication. Rather than the staff leading everything, the power would go back into the hands of the people.

I thought, *"Is there a name for that?"*

I didn't hear anything. I guess we got to name it.

So God said, *"You can have the standard megachurch thing, or you can have that other thing."*

"Well, God, I kind of like that movement thing. Let's go with that one!"

A little while later, God said to me, *"How would you feel if I took the building away?"* (God often speaks to me in questions or riddles.)

I literally sat up and said, "You're kidding, right?"

Silence.

So that same morning, I came to our offices and met with our staff and said, *"Umm… the Lord asked me a question this morning, and I think we need to prepare for the possibility that we're going to lose our building."*

Everyone just stared blankly at me, with that deer-in-the-headlights look.

"What we've got to do is really start to focus on these mid-sized Missional Communities, because if the building goes, they'll be the only things floating. There's nowhere else to go."

So we focused on that and put tons of energy into it. A year later, almost to the day, one of our tech guys was just checking with the local fire chief about some heaters, and the fire chief said, *"Hey, who said you could meet in here?"*

"Ahhh, I don't remember if anyone said we could, but no one said we couldn't. We did the city paperwork. They know we're here. It's all legal."

"You can't be here. It's illegal."

"What do you mean it's illegal?"

"The whole building is live. Electricity is shooting through the frame of the building. If anyone drilled through one of these walls, they would die."

"Well, how could we fix it?"

"Honestly? Knock it down."

"Knock it down?"

"Yep. Knock it down and rebuild it."

Sure, we could have fixed it, but we knew what God was asking of us. So one weekend shortly thereafter, the entire church was planted out across the city into dozens of Missional Communities. They met in garages, bowling allies, pubs, parks, houses, coffee shops, restaurants, schools, everywhere you could think of.

We nicknamed Sunday mornings "The Pony Express." The staff would gather early at the old parish church, and we'd take out tubs of children's supplies, Holy Communion, announcement sheets, and offering bags. Let's just say this wasn't the most systematized thing quite yet! It would become far more efficient and streamlined in the years to come, but at first, we were just trying to make it work. These MCs—groups of 20–50 people who all had one, focused mission together—were led by regular, ordinary members of the church.

Our job as the staff became equipping them and resourcing them. We let them lead and live into their calling. At the time, it was impossible to rent a space big enough to hold all of us each week, so we were able to get all of our MCs together only about every six weeks. It was invigorating and terrifying at the same time.

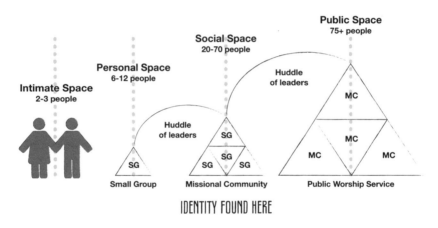

IDENTITY FOUND HERE

BUILDING A TEAM

In the midst of all the craziness of our church being homeless, the Lord did some powerful work in me in seeing how teams of movements can function.

As we've already covered, the team you have the opportunity to lead is meant to act as an *oikos*, functioning as an equipping body at the center of all that is happening around you. It is a true spiritual extended family. It isn't just the people you have serving in various capacities. It's their spouses, their kids. They are all part of the family.

One thing I've noticed is that the higher the challenge, and the more difficult your purpose on the missional frontier, the more you need time playing together. Movies. Dinners. Baseball games. Times to laugh, enjoy each other, and just be team apart from any higher purpose you have.

If we hadn't played as family during this year of being homeless, we wouldn't have survived.

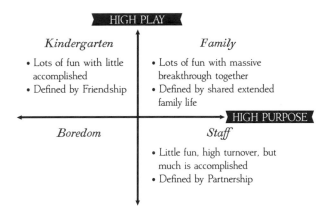

I can assure you that if you look at the great movements of the past (whether in business, politics, societal change, etc.), what you will find in the middle is a group of people truly living as an extended family.

It's not staff. It's family.

In an institution, your job is to look at the needs of the organization, figure out the specific roles that need to be filled, and then fill them. Just fill the role.

Although to a certain degree this remains true of a Kingdom movement, filling the roles doesn't happen exactly like that. Your first question isn't what roles need to be filled. Rather, it's, "Who is God calling to this team?" I am far more concerned with someone's character and whether he or she can hear the voice of God than I am about his or her competency.

I want to know who God is calling to join us in the family. But this is not a sentimental thing because although we are family, we are still a family of warriors who are going to battle together. Who are the people God wants me to be in the trenches with? It doesn't matter if you are gathering a team who will be paid or completely unpaid. It's your team. Your family.

The formation of a team is a lot like beginning a game of pool. Get all the balls on the table. Who are the ones God wants on this table? At first, these people are like pool balls on the table, sliding around, bumping up against each other. It feels like chaos.

But what happens pretty quickly is that the pressure of the mission (in a good way) starts to bear down on the team. Whereas before everyone was constantly bumping into each other, going this way and that, the call of purpose/mission serves as the "racker" that collects all the balls into a triangle. One at a time, they collect together into that triangle.

Then an amazing thing happens: They start to act as one. They are no longer autonomous, individual balls but a collection of balls going in one direction, this way or that, as they move together, in the racker, across the table.

During those times, I'm always paying close attention, as I want to notice how each ball works in the midst of the collective whole. In this time, I want to give them a new opportunity to reveal what they do. When given space, how do they function? I don't want them to function on what they believe their role says they should be; rather, I want to organize the team around where I see grace operating in each.

Originally, a ball might have thought it was the five ball. But as we discern together, we notice that it's not a five but a three. Because of that, I don't want to be too quick to assign detailed and specific roles and create intricate systems around them. All the things the team must accomplish, we must accomplish together. But we might not know until a little way down the road who will be doing what. We need to see grace at work first. Where is the grace?

Let's say we're organizing a baseball team, and someone promises up and down he's a second baseman. But as you observe, you notice he isn't actually the best second baseman. As you know about baseball, you don't do just one thing. There are several things you have to do: catching, throwing, hitting, stealing, running.

Seeing this, we make a switch. We send this person to the outfield during practice to see what happens. It turns out he isn't terribly good at that position either, and he doesn't hit well either. Now sometimes in practice it can get a little boring for outfielders, and this person brings a ball out. As he waits for a ball to be hit to him, he begins kicking the ball here and there, almost as if he were a hacky-sack pro. You watch in amazement at his deftness in kicking this ball and keeping it in the air.

As it turns out, it isn't that this person was in the wrong position. He was in the wrong sport. He is actually a soccer player!

You would be astonished at the number of times I've seen this metaphor play out in the teams I've formed over the years. People think they are this thing or that thing, but in reality, they are something else. They will play a crucial and pivotal role on the team, but in a different place than what they were originally thinking.

I know it sounds counter-intuitive, but this is what needs to happen when you form your team. Don't bring people on your team to fill roles. Bring people on your team because they are the people you believe God is calling to your team to be family.

God cares more about your team, your community, and Kingdom movements than you do. He will give you the people you need.

Organize around where you see the grace operating. Care more about the long-term sustainability and development of your team than the short-term success of the organization.

And remember that, in order for this to happen, you will probably have to experience some short-term failure, missteps, and frustration to ensure the long-term success of the team you're building. Know that going in. I'll say it again: You have to be more committed to the long-term life and viability of your team than you are to the short-term success of the organization. You don't get a movement without that.

WHERE IT LEADS

Now back to the story...

After more than a year of being without a building and being able to gather the whole congregation only every six weeks or so, the Lord gave us a large, industrial campus called Philadelphia. We turned those warehouses

into a worship space and training centers. But this time, the campus was built completely around equipping and resourcing disciples on mission.

With this campus, we were able to start meeting weekly again for people who wanted to worship as a whole community each week. Some MCs came every week, but some came only once a month or every other week. They worshipped in their MCs the other two or three weekends.

We had been homeless for more than a year, but a year later, the number of mid-sized Missional Communities had doubled. Each MC tried to reach into and incarnate themselves into a specific kind of network or neighborhood.

MCs for creative professionals.

MCs for the homeless.

MCs for parents with new babies.

MCs for Iranian Muslims.

MCs for artists.

MCs for people who worked at the same place or lived in the same neighborhood.

MCs for foreign students at the university.

5 DEFINING CHARACTERISTICS OF A MC:

1) **A group of 20-50 on mission together**

2) **Clear mission vision**

3) **Rhythms of UP/IN/OUT**

4) **Lightweight and Low Maintenance**

5) **Accountable leader**

We were reaching every kind of person you could imagine, seeing more people come to Christ as disciples than we could count. Then this incredibly diverse group of people would all gather and worship together once a month in a place big enough to hold us. As Lesslie Newbigin says, it was a sign and a foretaste of the coming, fulfilled Kingdom.[30] But we were experiencing it here and now.

Previously, our missional engagement was more about discipling people well so that they were released as individual missionaries in their everyday comings and goings. We always need this, of course. But now, we had focused communities of mission in which disciples were working in concert with each other. In other words, the missional force was so much stronger because it had the gravitational pull of an extended family (20–50 people).

Shortly thereafter, somewhere in the beginning of 2000, Christian Research (formerly MARC Europe), led by a brilliant statistician named Peter Brierley, released a report stating we had the largest attendance of any church in England, and probably the largest in Europe. The funny thing is… you'd never know it.

We had learned how to connect the **MESSAGE** of Jesus with the culture. We had learned to embrace the **MIRACULOUS**. But during this time, we came to understand the **METHOD** of the movement God was entrusting to us to steward.

---

[30] I'll point you to Newbigin's *Gospel in a Pluralist Society*.

6
∾ THE TWO TOWERS FALL ∾

Not long after that, like the rest of the world, I sat in stunned silenced when the Twin Towers fell to the ground on September 11, 2001. You don't know what to say; you don't know what to do. You just sit there. Watching. Glued to the television.

My wife, Sally, wasn't at home when it happened, so it was just me, and some of the staff team watching the TV in my house. We were in England (this happened before we moved to the United States), so it was in the afternoon there as it all started to unfold. After a while, I stood up and realized I was really shaken up. It was having quite the effect on me.

I sat there drinking a cup of tea, overwhelmed by it all, and suddenly I had this compulsion deep within my soul that we needed to pray. I don't say that in a trite way. The sense was overwhelming that we needed to gather and beg God on behalf of his children in America.

I picked up the phone and called each person in the Huddle I was discipling. All I said was this: "Call your guys (and girls, of course). Meet at the church at 7:00. We're going to pray."

That was it. That was all I said.

I sat back down and started to pray myself. I had another cup of tea, and 45 minutes later, it was getting close to 7:00. So I started walking toward the church. As I rounded the corner, I almost had to stop as I surveyed the scene. No one had opened the doors to the church yet, and hundreds and hundreds of people were waiting to get in. A somber but purposeful spirit permeated the crowd of people. I unlocked the doors, and we entered the worship space and began to pray. We prayed with a fervency that could move mountains. We begged God for his grace, mercy, and compassion. We prayed for hours and hours. We prayed deep into the night.

Eventually, we wrapped up and closed up the church. But as I was walking home, I thought to myself about the situation. I had simply called the people I was discipling, maybe seven or eight people, and somewhere between 300 and 400 people showed up. And not just normal "church people"—people who could do all of the things we read about in scripture. It was hundreds of people whose lives looked a lot like the life of Jesus.

The next day I talked to the people I was discipling, my team, and asked what they had done. They said, "We did exactly what you did. We called the people we were discipling and told them to call *their guys* and said to be at the church at 7:00 because we were going to pray. That was it."

Over the next few days and weeks, we started to trace out this phenomenon. This wasn't something we theorized about on paper and tried to make it work. We knew that *every disciple disciples* is one of the gospel imperatives of the Great Commission. But we took it seriously and created a culture where people discipling others could happen. **The church wasn't discipling all those people. This wasn't a corporate thing. People were discipling people.**

The theory simply emerged out of that reality, not the other way around.

REPRODUCTION

Movements are all about reproduction, and reproduction at every level.

- **DISCIPLES:** We need to reproduce people who look like Jesus.
- **VEHICLES:** We need reproducible vehicles for mission and discipleship that are lightweight and low maintenance.
- **CENTERS:** We need to reproduce missional sending centers that have the kind of spiritual mass into which people, families, and large groups of people can orbit.

Notice that the order of these is not accidental. Like an inverted pyramid, each builds on the one before. And in this, we see the rate-determining step for any Kingdom movement. Ultimately, what determines the success or failure of a movement?

If you can't multiply missional leaders, you're done. I don't know if I was ever that clear on this before the events from September 11 and the prayer service.

I realized it doesn't matter how good your vehicles are. It won't matter what kind of buildings you have or how much money you've got. If you don't know how to multiply leaders effectively, it will always be Kingdom growth by addition instead of by multiplication.

This thought was woven into Jesus' understanding of how the Kingdom of God works. For instance, he gave us a picture of a tree and said that good trees are supposed to bear good fruit. It's a simple picture, really. One tree can give you quite a lot of fruit. But it's more. In each piece of fruit is the seed of multiplication. Each piece of fruit has dozens of seeds that could produce more trees. And there wasn't just one piece of fruit on each tree, but *lots of fruit.*

So let's run this out:

- One tree
- One tree, hypothetically, has 100 pieces of fruit
- Each piece of fruit has, hypothetically, 20 seeds in it that can multiply into 20 more trees
- One tree = 2,000 potential trees

Multiplication is what Jesus is talking about in the Parable of the Sower. In another, you expect a return of 30, 60, 100 times what you invest with the one seed. It's multiplication.

Let's understand the context of what Jesus was going after. When Jesus talked about trees and fruit, he was referring to something very specific: *people.* He was saying that each person is a tree, and a disciple is someone who produces good fruit. If we take Jesus' metaphor seriously, he seems to be suggesting that a disciple will produce thousands of disciples.

If you're at all like me, that can seem incredibly daunting.

Then you realize where we started and do the simple math. You can't get there by addition, but you can by multiplication. We take what we've been given, invest it, and let it multiply.

Multiplication has been the way of the church for thousands of years because it was the way of Jesus.

The early church had two things going for it:

1. They had the Holy Spirit.
2. They knew how to multiply missional leaders.

That was it. No budgets, buildings, or any real cash on hand. All around there was moral relativism, polytheism, hedonism run amok, persecution, and an Empire that seemed to hate the church with a growing intensity.

And they blew the roof off!

At the end of the day, you could launch a missional movement with those same two things—the Holy Spirit and a way to multiply missional leaders. The problem is that many of us don't actually believe that.

If you were to go to Sheffield (which is now the epicenter of a worldwide missional and discipling movement), they would not tell you how many people attend the church. **I doubt most of the people would even realize how big the church is, because it doesn't function like one.**

If you asked how big the church is, they would simply tell you how many they are discipling. That is what they count. They count how many people are engaged in active, accountable, discipling relationships. Their whole structure for church is built around making disciples and releasing them. So that's what they count. That's the metric that matters. That's the Great Commission imperative.

How many disciples do we have?

St. Thomas Sheffield isn't a massive church and the center of a movement because it has the best worship service, or the best digital experience, or the best preachers or teachers in the world. It's because everything they do is about making disciples. They honestly believe that if you make disciples and release them to lead into their destiny, release them to be Agents of the Kingdom, everything will change.

If we are great at making the disciples, church growth will never be a problem, because being a disciple means you're a missionary. **It was never OK for us to be a large church and have very few missionary disciples. So we built something where that couldn't happen. Making disciples was in the DNA from the very beginning, and it has carried through into the movement of which it is the heart.**

LITTLE TREES, BIG TREES, + ORCHARDS

One of the images that's been playing in my mind the last few months is that of a large tree. But what I notice in approaching the tree and taking a closer look at it is that while the tree is quite large and has branches that are enormous, there is next to no fruit on the tree.

Conversely, there is a small tree a little ways off the beaten path, a tree not much larger than me, and the branches are still experiencing the growing pains between adolescence and adulthood. The tree is fairly young, but it has an inordinate amount of fruit, for the size of its branches and compared to the big tree.

So here's a question for you: If you had to pick between the big tree with little fruit or the little tree with lots of fruit, which one do you go with really? Not which one you know you're supposed to choose, but the one you actually do choose? Which one are you choosing now? Which one is your ministry telling you that you are choosing right now, at this very moment?

What Jesus tells us over and over again is to *follow the fruit*. Ruthlessly find the places where there is fruit (and as we just covered, when Jesus refers to fruit, he means *disciples*) and put every ounce of yourself in going after it. Having a big tree doesn't necessarily mean lots of disciples.

So let's be clear. If we are following Jesus, it means our ministries can never just be about the size of the tree. It has to be about the quality and quantity of the fruit. If you're all about the size of the tree, you really have to wonder if it's Jesus you're following. At the same time, we're not saying the tree isn't important. Large braches, strong trunks, help hold the fruit that God is producing instead of seeing that fruit fall off and rot quickly on the ground.

So here are a couple of questions for us. First, for those of us who have grown big trees (or at least spent the better part of our ministries trying to), will we learn from the small tree about how to bear a lot of fruit? Will we be humble enough to do that? Will we take on the posture of a learner? Will we be humble enough to do that? Or will we be content to have just a lot of people underneath our branches taking shade?

Second, for those of us who have begun chasing something different and have produced some fruit, will we take time to learn from the large tree? How did the branches grow to be so strong? How was their enough shade for so many? Will we put our skepticism and jealousy aside and choose to learn as well? Or will we just have a few people experiencing something profound that never really goes beyond them?

Here's the thing: At the end of the day, we don't want a small tree with a little fruit. We don't want a big tree with a little fruit. And we don't want just one big tree with a lot of fruit. *What we want is an orchard.*

We want reproduction on every level.

We want large, strong trees that bear tons of fruit, which can then produce more of the same. It's not about one tree, small or large. It's about producing an orchard with more fruit than we can wrap our minds around.

That's what a Kingdom movement is like.

ACROSS THE POND

Not long after we got into the new building, God made it quite clear to me that he wanted me to hand over the church to the young leaders I was discipling. The church wasn't mine to hold on to. God was absolutely clear this needed to happen.

The Lord told me Sally and I were supposed to leave.

"Where do you want me to go?"

Silence.

"Honestly. Where you do you want me?"

"Mike, we'll wait and see."

And that was the truth. Honestly, it was like a real Abrahamic call. One of my many pastor friends didn't understand at the time. He asked, "Why would you give up the church we all would want to pastor?"

All I knew was I supposed to go to America, and I would be shown what to do. In the years that followed, I was a coach, consultant, writer, practitioner, and speaker. I've worked with megachurches and church plants and everything in between.

There have been many times when it has felt like walking in the desert (a time that lasted seven years). To be honest, there were mornings when it was difficult to get up. I felt so unbelievably lost at times, not knowing exactly where to go or what would come next. Finally, God said, "This is it. This is what the rest of your life is going to be about." So we formed what we call 3DM, which simply is a movement of churches and missional leaders learning to put discipleship and mission at the center of everything, many of whom share the common language, practice, vehicles, and practices you're reading about in this book.

For us, it's not just theory.

If you make disciples, you really do get the rest. If you make disciples and release them, you will get new people entering the Kingdom. If you make disciples, you get the missional thing. If you make disciples, the places where society is torn in two and frayed at the edges start to be mended.

WORLDWIDE

Before we left Sheffield, a movement was afoot that started to spread far beyond the reach of the city of Sheffield. God was raising up a group of people who wanted to commit the entirety of their life to God's mission of redemption in the world. It's a fascinating thing, really. If you look at the whole of church history, what you find is that whenever a great awakening or revival swept through a place, it always began with a small group of people who radically committed themselves to discipleship and mission. In many ways, they are the tip of sword.

As Margaret Mead remarked, "Never doubt that a small group of thoughtful, committed [people] can change the world; indeed, it's the only thing that ever has."[31]

Often, these were monastic orders. They were people of whom you may have heard such as the Benedictines or Franciscans. As we listened to what God was saying to us, we discerned that he was asking for the formation of a similar group of people, that later would become an official order under the oversight of the Archbishop of York, though it welcomes members from all sorts of denominations. It is called The Order of Mission, and it is a group of people who live by a certain rule of life and who have taken vows of simplicity, accountability, and purity.

Some were paid ministers, but most were ordinary, everyday Christians who felt called to the mission of God wherever they found themselves. It had nothing to do with whether they were paid. They were called to be missionaries. Period.

Today, there are perhaps 600 members of The Order of Mission (TOM) on six continents, quietly living out movemental lives of discipleship and mission, connected to hundreds of thousands of people (at minimum). All this has come out of a sleepy city in England that most people have never heard of.

You see, eventually, movements take on a life of their own. TOM is certainly an example. Things have started to reproduce and multiply in places with which Sally and I have no contact.

We recently heard of a person in our movement who was ministering in a prison in the United States. For some strange legal reasons, he had to step

....

[31] Attributed to Margaret Mead in: Frank G. Sommers, Tana Dineen (1984) *Curing Nuclear Madness*. p.158.

away for a few months. When he returned four months later, there were now four *generations* of prisoners discipling other prisoners.

In the last six months, we've heard similar stories from Africa, Nepal, Scandinavia, Peru, Ecuador, Australia, Uganda, and the U.K. Scores of people are coming to faith from every tribe, nation and tongue.

I don't know about you, but where I'm from, we call that revival. And Sally and I aren't touching any of these places. It has taken on a life of its own. I love it.

Sometimes people talk about the book of Acts as if it's something that could never happen again. In part, they are right. But I think Jesus was quite serious when he said we would do greater things than he did. We see it in Acts. However, I also believe we will see greater things than we read about in the book of Acts. I believe it because I've seen it.

And I believe that is the story Jesus into which is inviting *all of us*.

PART 3

∽ THE JOURNEY ∽ WITHIN

Where we've been:

We've identified the world in which we find ourselves, one in the midst of seismic change but perfectly situated for a movement of a new kind of Reformation. I've given my own story as a backdrop for understanding some basic principles of a movement so we can better understand what might have been happening on a larger scale in the life of Paul.

Where we are going:

In Part 3, I want to show that any sustainable Kingdom movement starts in the heart of a leader. Does he or she have the character and competency to be a movement leader in the way that Jesus envisioned it? Certainly such character development doesn't happen overnight.

So what might this journey look like? First, we'll explore how this happened in the life of Paul. Then, we'll look to understand how he was able to sustain this work in his inner life against all odds.

7

∾ PAUL: ∾
A MAN WITH A MISSION

Not too long ago, a group of activists decided to change the world.

On our TVs, we watched the overthrow of several Middle Eastern governments because of the groundswell of a movement. Today, perhaps more so than at any other time, movements define the world in which we live.

MISSION:

The outward expression of your inward vision.

There have been many movements. The Berlin Wall came down not because of the decision of a government but because of a movement of freedom. Nelson Mandela didn't walk that mile from his cell to freedom because someone in a place of power decided it would happen. And the church in China didn't experience explosive growth in the last 50 years because the Chinese government changed its stance on Christianity.

Movements are what change the world.

We in the church represent the greatest movement the world has ever seen. Since the day of Pentecost, the movement of Jesus has been the most significant movement witnessed by humanity. But sometimes it feels like this movement is lying dormant.

Yet it is like a sleeping lion waiting to be roused.

In the 20th century, the power of the movement of Jesus was probably best seen among the Pentecostals. We are now about 100 years after the

Pentecostal movement began in Azusa Street in Los Angeles, California. The movement has seen hundreds of millions of people come into the Kingdom. We have watched as whole systems of poverty and injustice have been transformed as a result of this movement, particularly in places like South America and the Philippines.[32]

Movements are tremendously important to us.

From a sociological and anthropological point of view, history tells us why some movements are turning points for humanity. From time to time, the institutions on which we often rely and to which we sometimes cling are shaken by cultural upheaval and change. Since the resolution of the Second World War, the Western world has been under unprecedented stress. So it's no surprise that movements have continually pushed to the surface in these times. Like the images of liquefaction that we discussed earlier, the fluid elements of human community push to the surface, and everything starts moving.

We as leaders must learn how to lead movements serving the purposes of God within them. Unfortunately, that's not what usually happens. Most leaders, even younger leaders, are trained how to lead organizations, even institutions — but not movements. Of course, the world will not always move so violently, and in these times, a heavier hand of organizational and institutional leadership will be appropriate. But like the world Jesus found himself in, our world is on the move, and so we must learn these new skills to supplement the others already well tried and tested.

Thankfully, we have a biblical example in movement leading in the Apostle Paul.

WHAT IS YOUR MISSION, REALLY?

Paul was a man with a mission who eventually ended up with a movement.

But that's not where he started.

....

[32] To read how mid-sized groups within this kind of movement changed a slum of more than a million people in Manila, I definitely recommend *Companion to the Poor* by Viv Grigg.

He started simply with a mission—and a wrong mission at that. And it is in this humble beginning that we too are invited to begin creating a movement.

We know the story of Saul/Paul's conversion. He was on the road to Damascus on a mission, and the Lord Jesus metaphorically shook Paul by the shoulders. He was a man with a mission, *but it was the wrong mission*.

That has to give us hope, right? Paul went on to become one of the most extraordinary movement leaders the world has ever seen. But he didn't even start with the right mission. That's some good news for us!

Even after Jesus broke through, it took a period of re-orientation before Paul was pointed toward the movement he would lead.

Paul started in the wrong place. **I can't help but question whether we have the right mission.**

AND IN THE KINGDOM, you receive when you give. You live only when you die. You become free when you submit. You advance when you fully surrender.

Everyone has a mission. For some, the mission is success, money, stuff or the right spouse. For Christian leaders, the mission can often skew differently. It isn't money or stuff or 401(k)s. Rather, it can be the mission of a big church, of celebrity, of the affirmation of their leadership gifts or abilities. In such cases, the Kingdom of God is simply the thing on the side that might get a leader to his or her personal mission.

But this isn't about you. The Kingdom is the thing we seek above all else, forsaking all else, leaving all else.

Ultimately, we aren't after any old movement... we are after a *Kingdom movement*.

And in the Kingdom, you receive when you give. You live only when you die. You become free when you submit. You advance when you fully surrender.

This is the way of the Kingdom. And the mission is to see this *Kingdom* advance. Not our kingdom. Not a mission that is actually wrapped up in making sure we become celebrities, have the biggest church in town, or are constantly affirmed for our splendid gifts.

Your mission is simply the outward expression of the things that are most important to you. You might say that you want a Kingdom movement, but that doesn't mean your mission lines up with that. At the end of the day, if speaking on the main stage at a conference or having the most successful gig in town is what is most important to you, that is what will be expressed in your mission. No matter what kind of beautiful window dressing you give it, that's what will come out.

And you can't get a Kingdom movement with that. You just can't. *A Kingdom movement always begins in the heart of the leader.*

I can't help but wonder if there might need to be a radical reorientation of our hearts toward God's mission. *Do we have the right mission, or is it a mission different from that of the Kingdom?*

FROM MISSION TO MOVEMENT

Let's understand this about Paul: He had this radical reorientation. He now had a Kingdom mission, but it's not like a movement immediately dropped out of the sky. He had passion for the mission and immediately began preaching and seeking after the Kingdom. But the movement didn't materialize like that!

My guess is that, if you're reading this, you've got a mission. It may even be the right mission. But my guess is also that you don't find yourself part of or leading a movement.

Yet.

So let's briefly pick up Paul's story 13 years after his conversion to set the stage, and then make a quick U-turn to understand what got him to that place.

Acts 11:19-26

> *Now those who had been scattered by the persecution that broke out when Stephen was killed traveled as far as Phoenicia, Cyprus and Antioch, spreading the word only among Jews. Some of them,*

however, men from Cyprus and Cyrene, went to Antioch and began to speak to Greeks also, telling them the good news about the Lord Jesus. The Lord's hand was with them, and a great number of people believed and turned to the Lord.

News of this reached the church in Jerusalem, and they sent Barnabas to Antioch. When he arrived and saw what the grace of God had done, he was glad and encouraged them all to remain true to the Lord with all their hearts. He was a good man, full of the Holy Spirit and faith, and a great number of people were brought to the Lord.

Then Barnabas went to Tarsus to look for Saul, and when he found him, he brought him to Antioch. So for a whole year Barnabas and Saul met with the church and taught great numbers of people. The disciples were called Christians first at Antioch.

Here, we have a look at the first spontaneous outburst of the Kingdom of God beyond Jerusalem and the Holy Land. Thirteen years earlier, on the day of Pentecost, the church exploded and gained thousands of new converts. Acts 2 shows the kind of lifestyle that was so attractive and compelling to those who came in contact with the people who followed The Way. Teachings. Wonders. Signs. Miracles. Temple. Home. Breaking bread. Common life. Shared property. They didn't seek to hold onto anything themselves.

That community grew in influence, and the local religious leaders grew increasingly worried and insecure. So they put to death Stephen, one of the early leaders of the church. (It's worth noting that his leadership, according to Acts 6, was waiting on tables because the apostles could not neglect the ministry of teaching the word.) Stephen was truly an amazing, godly person.

He was stoned after he gave his defense of the gospel in showing how all of history points to Jesus as Messiah and Son of God. They stoned him, and a young man, probably no more than 30 years old, was holding the coats of those who threw the rocks.

Acts 8:1-3

> On that day a great persecution broke out against the church in Jerusalem, and all except the apostles were scattered throughout Judea and Samaria. Godly men buried Stephen and mourned deeply for him. But Saul began to destroy the church. Going from house to house, he dragged off both men and women and put them in prison.

Some of these words are tremendously important for us in understanding the work of Paul (still called Saul, at this point). He began the persecution by moving from the public space to the social space. Of course, the public space, in sociological terms, is the large place of interaction where people often gather for encouragement, inspiration, and entertainment. My godson recently went to see Coldplay with 20,000 other people. That's a public space event. It's designed to engage and inspire.

The public space is not needed all the time, but for human beings to function well, we need to gather in these larger groups to be inspired and encouraged to continue journeying in the beliefs and values that we espouse. The public space reminds you of the connecting story you are part of, of the "metanarrative" that drives your life.

The social space is, by and large, the most important space because it is where human beings find identity. It is a group of 20–70 people, and it is the place of extended family. Anthropologists tell us that if you leave human beings alone for long enough, this is what they re-create[33]—a group of blood and non-blood relationships who become their extended family.

....

[33] For more on this, see E.T. Hall's theory on proxemics or Joseph Myers' *The Search to Belong*.

The early church had public space worship in the Temple, at Solomon's Colonnade, and social space gathering in the homes. (Remember that homes in this period were not built for nuclear families but for extended families.) The Greek word used in Acts 2:46 for this is *oikos*—the household.

Of course, within the social space you have the personal space (up to 12 people, usually made up of the nuclear family) and the intimate space (two to three people, usually found in marriage).[34]

All of this works a bit like a Russian *matryoshka* doll. Each space fits within the other.

If the public space becomes the target of persecutors, clearly it shuts down. People move underground, and exist only in groups of 20–70, in the *oikos*. This is what happened in Jerusalem. The temple became a no-go area for followers of Jesus. Saul had seen that this persecution had been successful in public, and so he directed his attack where people were still gathering: the homes.

Acts 8:3. *But Saul began to destroy the church. Going from house to house, he dragged off both men and women and put them in prison.*

He went from house to house, dragging off believers and taking them to prison. Now by the end of the story you'll see Paul going from house to house, doing something else entirely.[35] But at this point, Paul was a man with a mission: destroy the church.

In that destructive desire, he was able to do two things: one he wanted, one he didn't. First, he was able to locate communities in the homes. He seemed to have success finding these early Christians. But something else happened. *They scattered.* **This was definitely not what he was hoping for.**

The word scattered pops up again a little later in the story.

....

[34] For a more thorough examination of the Four Spaces, please see my earlier work *Launching Missional Communities: A Field Guide*.

[35] Acts 20:20. Paul speaking, in giving an account to the Ephesian elder: "You know that I have not hesitated to preach anything that would be helpful to you but have taught you publicly and from house to house."

Acts 11:19. "Those who were *scattered* went to Antioch." Christians from Cyprus and North Africa (Cyrene)—two Jewish communities that were closely related—began to share their faith story with Gentiles as well as Jews.[36]

When the church heard that people were sharing the gospel with Gentiles, they sent one of their own, a man from Cyprus, to figure out what was going on. This was a strategy the church always used when it had difficulty with different ethnic groups in the church. In Acts 6, when the Greek-speaking Jews felt their widows were being overlooked in the daily food distribution, they gathered a group of Greek-speaking leaders to sort it out.

That's just smart.

So off went Joseph, a Levite from Cyprus known as Barnabas (a nickname meaning "son of encouragement"). He saw the amazing thing that God was doing in Antioch as Greek-speaking Gentiles came to faith in droves.

I imagine at this point something tweaked his memory. "Was it as long as 13 years ago that that young Pharisee met Jesus on the road to Damascus? Didn't Jesus tell him he'd be a witness to the Gentiles? Didn't I take that young guy and introduce him to the apostles? And didn't the apostles say, 'You're too hot right now, too radioactive, you need to go somewhere other than here?' Where was he from? Oh yeah... Tarsus. Well, that's not very far from here. I could probably walk there in a week."[37]

So Barney decided to go find that young man who had disappeared all those years ago.

SHAKEN TO SECLUSION

Barnabas knew that once Paul came to faith in Jesus, he began stirring up all kinds of problems in Damascus sharing his faith. He barely escaped death. He had to be lowered in a basket down the wall of one of the gates of the city. He went to Jerusalem, getting passage through Barnabas, who vouched for

---

[36] There's a great book I'll reference a few times on the story of John Mark that digs into this part of church history and beyond: Thomas Oden's *The African Memory of Mark*.

[37] Acts 11:22-26

him. He spent time with the apostles, particularly Peter, for about 15 days. Finally, they told him he needed to go somewhere else.[38]

So what happened next?

What happens next is a series of terrors. In 2 Corinthians 11:23-29, Paul gives a clear catalogue of much of what happens in those nine to 13 *hidden years*. (There's some debate among scholars about how long that period was, but I'd place it around 10 years.)

> *Are they servants of Christ? (I am out of my mind to talk like this.) I am more. I have worked much harder, been in prison more frequently, been flogged more severely, and been exposed to death again and again. Five times I received from the Jews the forty lashes minus one. Three times I was beaten with rods, once I was pelted with stones, three times I was shipwrecked, I spent a night and a day in the open sea, I have been constantly on the move. I have been in danger from rivers, in danger from bandits, in danger from my fellow Jews, in danger from Gentiles; in danger in the city, in danger in the country, in danger at sea; and in danger from false believers. I have labored and toiled and have often gone without sleep; I have known hunger and thirst and have often gone without food; I have been cold and naked. Besides everything else, I face daily the pressure of my concern for all the churches. Who is weak, and I do not feel weak? Who is led into sin, and I do not inwardly burn?*

We know that a few of these things happen *after* this period in his life, but most of Paul's description here occurred during these hidden years.

What can we discern from this?

First of all, Paul got himself into some real trouble.

Receiving the 40 lashes minus one was the most severe penalty that could be given by a synagogue court except stoning. Here's the thing: it was almost

---

[38] Galatians 1:18-20

always given as a sign of excommunication from the synagogue. Paul had been excommunicated from his people on five separate occasions. He had also run into the Roman authorities twice. The *lictors* who stood behind the Roman magistrate with the great bundles of rods were the administrators of Roman justice. To exercise this justice, they would lay the prisoner down, take out a rod, and beat the prisoner on the legs and back with the rod, flaying the skin and sometimes breaking bones.

We know that Paul went to Tarsus, his hometown, after his time in Jerusalem.[39] Knowing Paul, I can't imagine a scenario where he didn't preach the gospel there. Given this, we can be almost fully sure that this is one of the synagogues that excommunicated him. The early church memory tells us that his family had abandoned him because of this excommunication.

We can be just as certain that his wife divorced him during this time. Yes, Paul was almost certainly married. It is almost inconceivable that a Pharisee would be given the kind of responsibility given to Paul in persecuting the church if he weren't married. *It would never happen.*

When Barnabas came to look for Paul, his family had abandoned him. His wife was gone, and probably his kids too. Everyone who knew him counted him as dead. We know that he tried to plant churches during this period, and it appears he had next to no success.

Now what we discover from many of the early church fathers is that while Paul was utterly broken physically, Barnabas found him in a cave in the Taurus mountains, out of the reach of those in Tarsus wanting to find him. And there, as a lonely hermit, Paul was probably wondering what had happened to the mission Jesus had given him.

Due to many beatings, his legs would have been bandy (when your legs irregularly turn outward at the knees). He was stooped and bent over, not able to straighten his back. This is common among those who have suffered the systematic tortures Paul suffered. The scar tissue on his back would heal after the previous beating, only to be ripped open with the next whipping, creating the scar tissue that built up and warped his back with each successive beating.

....

[39] Acts 9:30

You can get a visceral picture of what he probably looked like if you think of Quasimodo.[40] He would have needed to strain his neck up just to make eye contact, compensating for a back bending at a 60-degree angle. Once a vital man with a mission, Paul was no more than 43 years old living in a cave with a broken failing body and a track record of apparent failures. He was socially isolated, and cut off from his family, without wife or children.

In every way we can think about it, Paul was a failure.

More than likely, he had given up. Seriously. He'd given up.

And wouldn't you? For most people, that would have been the end of their mission.

But then Barney shows up.

Barnabas came to Paul's cave and said, "Son, it's happening! It's *really* happening. All that you had in your heart that day on the road to Damascus… it's happening. Gentiles are coming to faith!" All the pain and opposition and abandonment must have made Paul think that he had gotten it wrong. But no! It was happening![41]

The Holy Spirit was stirring the Gentile population. And though stooped and broken and bowlegged, Paul followed Barnabas back into the harvest.

What had been a night of weeping now became a dawn of joy.

The tears that he had shed had watered the seeds of faith, and the Kingdom on earth was growing. It was happening. And for a whole year, it was harvest time in Antioch as Barnabas and Paul served there. The mission began to roll, and the great flywheel of God's purposes began to move.

Paul had lived out what the psalmist describes in Psalm 103. "Praise the Lord, my soul, and forget not all his benefits—who forgives all your sins and heals all your diseases, who redeems your life from the pit and crowns you with love

....

[40] From the book *The Hunchback of Notre Dame*

[41] Acts 11:25-26

and compassion, who satisfies your desires with good things so that your youth is renewed like the eagle's." He found himself in the pit. Desolate. Alone. Feeling rejected. Surrounded. But in the pit, the Lord gave Paul something: the gold that is always revealed in times of suffering and pain. What we see in Paul is someone who stayed in the pit long enough to mine out the gold and then see how God fashioned it into a crown of compassion.[42] **Something was shaped in the heart and character of Paul that created the space for everything that was to come.**

I wonder if there are words that God spoke to you long ago that feel dormant. Maybe even dead. I wonder if you are reminded of the great anticipation you once had to be part of God's Kingdom. And if you find yourself in your own pit, your own cave, what are you looking for?

And if you've come out of the pit, I wonder what God shaped in you. I wonder how that experience will release a movement of redemption, restoration, and healing for untold numbers of people.

....

[42] Psalm 103:4: "Who redeems your life from the pit and crowns you with love and compassion."

8

∾ PAUL: ∾
MESSAGE

Acts 13:1-3

Now in the church at Antioch there were prophets and teachers: Barnabas, Simeon called Niger, Lucius of Cyrene, Manaen (who had been brought up with Herod the tetrarch) and Saul. While they were worshiping the Lord and fasting, the Holy Spirit said, "Set apart for me Barnabas and Saul for the work to which I have called them." So after they had fasted and prayed, they placed their hands on them and sent them off.

MESSAGE:
Communicating outwardly what you have experienced inwardly so that others can receive it transformationally.

Paul was once in the demolition business, but now he was in the building business. Destruction becomes construction. When we first saw him in Acts 8, his mission was to destroy the church, going from house to house and demolishing the church. So it is interesting that he later described himself as a builder. At one end, he was a man with a wrecking ball; at the other, he was a man with a trowel. At one end, he held a sledgehammer, at the other a hammer and mallet.

As we have seen, Jesus accosted Paul on the road to Damascus, and Paul probably spent 13 years with nothing to show for it. In the end, Barnabas found Paul, and they spent a year of incredible harvest in Antioch, the place where believers were first called Christians.

Other leaders of the church in Antioch, along with Paul and Barnabas, started to gather regularly. The text indicates that structure was emerging. The church had leaders. It also seems to suggest very matter-of-factly that worship and prayer were regular routines for these leaders. In movements, spontaneity always gives rise to some loose governing structure, in the same way that structure must always give rise to spontaneity. Neither is sustainable without the other.

CONTINUUMS, NOT COMPARTMENTS

Organization was beginning to emerge. It isn't that things are either ORGANIC or ORGANIZED. These things don't exist in compartments; rather, they always co-exist on a continuum. The same is true of STRUCTURE and SPONTANEITY. It seems that after a year of a great harvest in Antioch, there was a need to spend time focusing on structure and organization. Not to the point where things became hardened and inflexible, but to the point where organization and structure could support all the life that was being birthed.

It's a delicate balance, that one.

The more we think about continuums and the less we think about compartments, the more effective we will be at leading movements. (We aren't going to talk about all that quite yet, but it's coming.)

Paul and Barnabas launch into their mission.

We sometimes forget that Barnabas was the leader right now. He was the elder and the one who was more mature and experienced, and they went to his "Jerusalem"—his home in Cyprus. Jesus had made it clear that you go to Jerusalem, Judea, Samaria, and then the ends of the earth. So they began their mission not in some foreign land but among the people Barnabas already knew.

You don't become a missionary by buying a plane ticket. You begin with the people you know. And if you do OK there, then you go a little further, to your Judea. And if that works out, a little further. You see how it works.[43]

....

[43] For more exposition of this concept, please see Chapter 5 of my book *Multiplying Missional Leaders*.

Paul and Barnabas came into the eastern port, across the island to the farthest western outpost and worked in the synagogues.

Why in the Jewish synagogue? Barnabas (whose real name was Joseph) was a Levite who had high status and religious credentials. Paul, too, having been trained by the famous Rabbi Gamaliel, had excellent religious credentials. So they began where they could use their credentials most effectively.[44]

It is not as if Paul forgot about the Gentiles. It's simply that Barnabas was in charge, and so they went to Barnabas's version of Jerusalem and walked through the first door available.

They went to the synagogue to present Jesus as Messiah. Finally, they ended up in front of Sergius Paulus, the proconsul of Cyprus who came to faith after Paul cursed his sorcerer with blindness.[45]

Then they left Cyprus to travel on.

....

[44] Acts 4:36-37
[45] Acts 13:11-12

TEXT AND CONTEXT

Acts 13:13-16

> *From Paphos, Paul and his companions sailed to Perga in Pamphylia, where John left them to return to Jerusalem. From Perga they went on to Pisidian Antioch. On the Sabbath they entered the synagogue and sat down. After the reading from the Law and the Prophets, the leaders of the synagogue sent word to them, saying, "Brothers, if you have a word of exhortation for the people, please speak." Standing up, Paul motioned with his hand and said: "Fellow Israelites and you Gentiles who worship God, listen to me!*

This is fascinating. What Paul then said here is almost exactly what he had heard 14 years earlier from the lips of Stephen. Remember, when Paul heard Stephen's message, Paul was on the other team. When those who wanted to throw stones at Stephen needed someone to hold their coats, Paul was the man for the job. It wasn't that Paul didn't want to throw a rock; it was that he was a young man and didn't have sufficient status within the community to do so yet. But he openly identified himself with executing the sentence of death.

It's interesting that the words of Stephen had settled in Paul's heart. The Lord was already at work in Paul as he listened to Stephen, and these words stuck with him, found root, and eventually bore fruit.

Here in Pisidian Antioch, Paul shared Stephen's panoramic view of scripture, placing John the Baptist and Jesus within it, and locating the gospel in the death and resurrection. Thankfully for Paul and Barnabas, the people warmly embraced the good news.

This was great, but in Paul, something else was beginning to emerge. Paul was bringing text and context together. He was a skilled and logical rhetorician, but he had been trained in first-century Judaism. Here, he applied those skills and his extensive learning to a new context.

Paul had a calling to the Gentiles, but he had to learn how to contextualize his message to that culture. Just because you've been called to a group of people doesn't mean you have a clue how to contextualize the message of Jesus well. In fact, you could be really bad at it. What Paul found (and we see clearly in the life of Jesus) is you do this by bringing TEXT and CONTEXT together.

Most people have a tendency toward one or the other. If we are Context people, then we are all about Relevance. We've seen the emergence of the gospel of Relevance across the Western world. We've tried as many ways as we can to make the Good News relevant and boiling it down to its essential elements, making those elements as understandable as possible. We do this so people can hear it. If our principle focus is context, Relevance is our overarching emphasis.

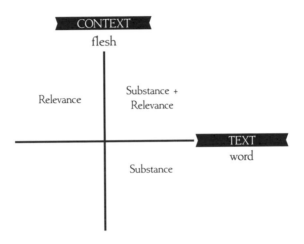

On the other hand, if we have a proclivity to mainly focus on the Text, then we tend to emphasize Substance. The great debates in evangelicalism today often revolve around two warring parties emphasizing these different things. It's Substance vs. Relevance. Deep vs. Wide.

One says: "Well, we need to PREACH THE WORD in season and out of season."

Another says: "Man, we've just got to make it relevant. That's why I wear such tight jeans and a V-neck T-shirt. Don't you see how it makes the gospel more understandable?" (kidding)

Of course the truth is found in the tension between the two. As my friend Dave

Rhodes puts it, "The answer to polarity is almost always paradox."

Paul's original Context was the Jews. And even though he was now called to the Gentiles, he always honored his heritage by beginning with God's chosen people. As he engaged with his mission, he did so with a new context. On the island of Cyprus, it was clear that the Lord was anointing, empowering, and equipping Paul to take the baton of leadership from Barnabas and lead the team himself, as God gave him favor to reach Gentiles.

As we mentioned earlier, on Cyprus Paul encountered the governor of the island. Starting at Acts 13:6:

> They traveled through the whole island until they came to Paphos. There they met a Jewish sorcerer and false prophet named Bar-Jesus, who was an attendant of the proconsul, Sergius Paulus. The proconsul, an intelligent man, sent for Barnabas and Saul because he wanted to hear the word of God. But Elymas the sorcerer (for that is what his name means) opposed them and tried to turn the proconsul from the faith.

(This indicates that Sergius Paulus was orienting his heart toward Jesus.)

> Then Saul, who was also called Paul, filled with the Holy Spirit, looked straight at Elymas and said, "You are a child of the devil and an enemy of everything that is right! You are full of all kinds of deceit and trickery. Will you never stop perverting the right ways of the Lord? Now the hand of the Lord is against you.

Paul knew what it was like to have the hand of the Lord against him. He knew what it was like for the Lord to oppose the proud and give grace to the humble. On the road to Damascus, when he was a man full of pride, the hand of the Lord was opposed to him. He was knocked off his horse and struck blind.

Clearly, Paul had faith for what was about to happen. Like so many of us, Paul had faith for things that he had experienced himself.

> "You are going to be blind for a time, not even able to see the light of the sun."

Immediately mist and darkness came over him, and he groped about, seeking someone to lead him by the hand. When the proconsul saw what had happened, he believed, for he was amazed at the teaching about the Lord. From Paphos, Paul and his companions sailed to Perga in Pamphylia, where John left them to return to Jerusalem.

What is this telling us? It is telling us that Paul, a Jewish Pharisee who had struggled against impossible odds, who had been excommunicated from five synagogues, who had been shipwrecked, who had been in danger in all kinds of circumstances, and who had been alienated and alone. Saul, the believing Pharisee, had now become an apostle to a new context. So he took on a new name, a new identity.

Chances are that "Paul" was one of the names given to him at his circumcision. His parents were Roman citizens with high status who thus had various Latin and Greek names, identifying them with different groups. "Paul" was probably one of his names.

But proconsul Sergius Paulus served as an indication of the fulfillment of the promise that Jesus gave Paul on the road to Damascus: Governors and the kings of the Gentiles would hear the witness of the gospel through him.[46] The governor of Cyprus had become a disciple of Jesus, and his name was Paul. And so Saul took the name Paul as Barnabas passed the baton of leadership to him. Effectively, Barnabas was saying, "You lead, I'll follow. Where are we going next?"

And so, they went to a place familiar to Paul. They couldn't go to Tarsus. He was *persona non grata* there. So he went to Pamphylia, near the region of Galatia, perhaps the most dangerous place in the whole of the Roman Empire.

Paul was still working out what he was supposed to do among the Gentiles. He continued to speak in the synagogues first. But he began to hone his message, making it more contextual to the people there, knowing that in every synagogue, there was a section designated for the God-fearing Gentiles.

....

[46] Acts 9:15 speaks of this future for Saul/Paul.

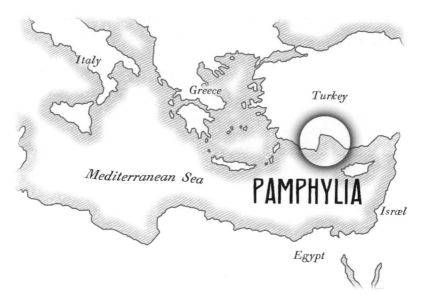

By the time we get to Acts 17, we find Paul in Athens. There has been much speculation about whether Paul was ever really successful in Athens. But such a suggestion of failure to me is complete rubbish! He left a church behind! You can approach success any way you want. But to me, if you leave a church behind at the epicenter of Gentile philosophical thought, you've done something pretty remarkable! And he did it after only a few weeks. Paul had become the contextual missionary *par excellence*.

ANTHROPOLOGY + ARTIFACTS

Paul got into all kinds of shenanigans as he went to Europe for the first time. By the time he arrived in Athens, he didn't have his team with him; he had left them at past stops or sent them off to various churches, some to oversee, some to continue the process of planting. He arrived in Athens and did the work that all missionaries should do—*the work of an amateur anthropologist*.

If you want to be a good missionary to Holland, you have to be an anthropologist. If you want to be a missionary to Ohio, you've got to do the work of an anthropologist. It doesn't matter if it's New York, New Zealand, Delhi, or Denmark. You have to do it.

What do I mean by anthropologist? I mean you need to become someone who observes context and culture. When you observe context, you observe culture. And when you look at culture, you ask yourself a few questions.

What does this culture make? And what do the things this culture makes tell me about what these people believe?

These things are called *artifacts*.

What are the *artifacts* of this culture, and what do they say to me?

As a missionary for some time to England, I've had to embrace various subcultures within the wider culture. One of the particular calls Sally and I had was reaching out to a very forgotten generation in the European church called Generation X. That's pretty much everyone born from 1960 to 1980. Of course, Sally and I deeply love these folks, but they are an absolute nightmare! They were born into the cultural upheaval of the 1960s, and their world was shaken to its very foundation. This forced them to clear away the rubble of the culture they found. All this rubble-clearing amply equipped them to be superb deconstructionists. Having been born into the upheaval, they see the rubble of the cultural earthquake they try to clear it and then ask, "OK, what's left now?" What's left? More deconstruction, of course!

Generation Y, those born between 1980 and 2000, is filled much more with people who were born after the first shock of the cultural earthquake, ask, "Hey, what do you think we could build with all this rubble?" They are postmodern like Gen X, but it's astonishing how different these two generations are. Generation Y actually has a positive view of life. They are not as concerned with deconstruction as the Xers, but are far more concerned with construction. Whether they are Christians or not, you could genuinely call Gen Y a *missional* generation because they want to build something good in this world.

I look at Generation X and the artifacts they create. I look at their number one TV show from the 1990s (*Friends*) and ask:

- Have they given up on the Western nuclear family?
- Have they given up on family as the cornerstone of security and existence?

Although Gen Xers are still governed by the drives of all humans to raise and nurture children, they do this with all kinds of internal conflicts. Gen Xers seem to genuinely distrust the institutions of marriage and family and, as the artifacts suggest, build their primary relational identity with people who are friends and not blood relatives.

Interestingly enough, the number one show right before *Friends* was the one defined by the Boomers: *Home Improvement*. It was a classic Boomer statement: "We know the family isn't that great—let's try to fix it." Whereas Gen X looked at things and said, "Nah. It's all fallen down. Let's just give up on it."

Now the TV shows that in many ways tell the story of Gen Y and their desire for reconstruction are called *Modern Family* and *Parenthood*—both about an extended family. They are all mad as hatters (that is what makes it so funny), but it is compelling television.

These TV shows are artifacts of different generational cultures.

Being an amateur anthropologist was important in my call to be a missionary to Generation X. This was brought home to me when I heard about *The Blair Witch Project*, one of the biggest films of the 1990s. It popularized, in a whole new way, how the camera sees the world. Not a lot of Christians were too excited about it. But on Sunday before it was released, in front of our congregation, I said, "I'm going to *The Blair Witch Project*. Anyone want to come?"

Silence.

Jaws slightly ajar.

Eyes glancing around from person to person.

"Did the vicar just say that?"

My sense in praying about it was that there was something powerful for understanding this generation that was to be found in this movie. There was no sex. No violence. No swearing. It was a modern retelling of Hansel and Gretel—children lost in a forest and a witch who is going to devour them. The witch is an unseen, malevolent force that creates massive anxiety.

I wondered, "Is that really what Gen Xers think about life?"

So I did a little statistical digging. Half the people in Gen X believe they will die an untimely death. The single most important "internal" issue for this generation is stress and fear. They believe that they are children, without parents, lost in a forest that they thought would fulfill their dreams, and that they are being stalked by a malevolent evil out to kill them.

I came to church the next Sunday and shared my insights, and said, "I think this is what Gen Xers believe about life and the movie said to me—but there is a gospel for this, and this is it: There is one who has lived, died, and is risen again who can deliver you from that malevolent force, one who can give you peace in the place of your anxiety. If you want to meet your rescuer, come forward."

At the time, the church where I was Team Rector met at Ponds Forge, a local sports center. It was a huge gym with the worst echo you can possibly imagine. I can still hear the sound in my ears. It sounded like a waterfall that grew until it was like a mighty rushing river because hundreds of people came forward, stepping down from the bleachers. Hundreds. We had so many people we didn't know what to do with them.

Why? Because the message was contextualized.

Paul in Athens said this: "People of Athens! I see that in every way you are very religious. For as I walked around and looked carefully at your objects of worship, I even found an altar with this inscription: *to an unknown god*. So you are ignorant of the very thing you worship—and this is what I am going to proclaim to you."[47]

This is how you do contextual mission: You find a way of connecting the Text to the Context. You find that connection by first finding the gap in the worldview. For Paul, the gap was that these people were incredibly religious and bowed their knees to an untold number of idols in the hope that

....

[47] Acts 17:22-23

they would appease the capricious gods and make it through life with some kind of hope and satisfaction.

Their anxiety ran deep: "But what if we haven't worshipped *all of the gods*, and we missed one? What if there is an unknown god we haven't worshipped, and he/she/it is really upset with us? What if it comes for our life?"

An incomplete worldview comes with inbuilt anxiety. (And just a little clue here—no one has a complete worldview.) When you find the incompleteness in the worldview, there is an opportunity for hope, peace, and redemption. What Paul did was speak to the leaders of the Greco-Roman world and present to them a gospel that began with their own philosophy. He used their language and couched the gospel in words and vocabulary that they would understand. He took them on a journey and led them into a story where only one god could cure the maladies of their collective anxiety.

He spoke about the resurrection with the intent of taking them to the cross. But when he got there, they stopped and said, "Resurrection? We'll hear more on this some other time." They cut in on him, but something did happen: Persons of Peace were revealed—people God had prepared in advance for the gospel. They heard Paul and asked to hear more.[48]

In his work as a contextual missionary, Paul became amazingly adept at cultural anthropology, at recognizing the worldview, finding the gap, and zeroing in with the gospel.

If you're going to be effective in Ohio, Norway, Toledo, Toronto, Peru, Nepal, or Sheffield, wherever—you're going to have to find a way to contextualize the text of scripture with the part of the world the Lord has given you to reach. At first, contextualization appears a very complex thing, but it is at the heart of discipleship.

Jesus redefined "the wise person" as his disciple. At the end of his great Sermon on the Mount, the wise person who built his house on the rock is the one who listens to Jesus and puts it into practice. Listening, attending to the words of Jesus, and putting them into practice is exactly what it means to be a disciple.

....

[48] Acts 17:32

As I have said many times before, discipleship revolves around answering two questions: "What is God saying to us?" "What are we going to do about it?"

Of course, we need to be disciples before we become a missionary. You simply can't be a missionary if you're not a disciple, first and foremost. It's impossible. But the natural outgrowth for any disciple of Jesus is the life of a missionary.

Fortunately, the skills of listening to and applying the word of Jesus really help us in the fundamental task of being a missionary. If we want to understand what it is to be a missionary, we only need to look to how John talks of Jesus in John 1:14: *The Word becomes **flesh** and **dwells** among us.*

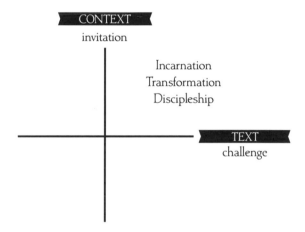

Incarnational mission requires the same internal and external process as radical discipleship and contextualizing our message.

9

～ PAUL: ～
METHOD

For Sally and me, learning to contextualize the message to our mission field was only part of the calling. We needed to find a methodology for being the church as well. I find it interesting that during our time in Sheffield we learned so much about communication and community. This was very similar to Paul.

What was Paul's methodology? Well, we know all the broad brushstrokes. He operated in each location he visited by going into the synagogue, starting first with the Jewish people, and then expanding to the Gentiles. But beyond that, was there something Paul learned along the way?

Let's backtrack a little to understand this.

METHOD:
The most reproducible Kingdom practice that results in the most significant Kingdom progress.

On the day of Pentecost, the church numbered about 3,120 people. Of course, that included 120 disciples in an Upper Room, plus the 3,000 who came to faith at Pentecost. A pretty simple math equation.

At the time of the stoning of Stephen, the church may have measured 20,000. Then persecution broke out, and it continued in waves, off and on in presence and severity, for the next three centuries. In those next 250 years, that small group of 120 people, huddled in a room waiting for the Holy Spirit, turned into the most powerful movement the world had ever seen.

You and I are the beneficiaries and torchbearers of this very same movement.

To put numbers to it, in that span of three centuries, framed by the Edict of Milan in AD 313, those 120 people launched a movement that would add up to more than 50 percent of the Roman Empire. Move forward to today, and billions of people are disciples of Jesus.[49]

Clearly, we understand the Holy Spirit was the main force in all of this, and we will discuss that a little later. But what we also need to understand is that the Holy Spirit doesn't tend to work in chaotic and unpredictable ways. Rather, the Spirit works in concert with us so that the Kingdom can unfold in a way in which we play a part.

In other words, we can never lose sight of the Holy Spirit power in all of Paul's work; but it's also important to understand the methodology that he discovered as he watched the Spirit at work.

That's because this methodology, discovered by Paul, saw Christianity become the astonishing movement that not only survived persecution, polytheism, secularism, moral relativism, and a brutal Empire; but that also, even more, became the movement that *transform*ed the world.

So let's return to the beginning, because in many ways it is here that God reveals the DNA that Paul would discover, repeat, and pass on to others.

Acts 2:42-47

> *They devoted themselves to the apostles' teaching and to fellowship, to the breaking of bread and to prayer. Everyone was filled with awe at the many wonders and signs performed by the apostles. All the believers were together and had everything in common. They sold property and possessions to give to anyone who had need. Every day they continued to meet together in the temple courts. They broke bread in their homes and ate together with glad and sincere hearts, praising God and enjoying the favor of all the people. And the Lord added to their number daily those who were being saved.*

....

[49] See Rodney Stark's excellent work *The Rise of Christianity*.

Many people have written and taught sermons on the four legs of early Christianity found in verse 42 and how, when we rely on them, they will keep us grounded and stable:

- Devotion to teaching
- Devotion to fellowship
- Devotion to breaking of bread
- Devotion to prayer

But in verse 46, the Holy Spirit emphasizes something that I believe is of equal importance. It is not simply what the disciples believed or embraced, but the continuum on which all of their life was conducted. What was this continuum of life in which these early believers embraced teaching, fellowship, the breaking of bread, and prayer?

Acts 2:46. *Every day they continued to meet together in the temple courts. They broke bread in their homes and ate together with glad and sincere hearts.*

It was something they did *every single day*.

We have already seen this in sociological terms. We can say that the early church embraced a continuum of behavior that lived in the public space (a group of 75 or more people) and the social space (a group of 20–70 people). They lived in the extended family, the *oikos*, the home, but also in the Temple, where public worship inspiration and teaching took place.

Clearly, some things can happen in each space that cannot happen as well in the other. That's just how the social dynamics that govern group size work.

In the public space, we are able to be inspired. We can gather as a tribe. There are all kinds of ways of doing teaching and worship that aren't available in a smaller group. With that comes a level of organization that allows people to engage with this gathering without it being chaotic and confusing.

This reality reveals to us that we can put other words on our continuum.

TEMPLE	HOME
Organized	Organic

Clearly a level of organization was still needed when 20–70 people gathered in these early church households, but a level of organic life also existed compared to gathering thousands of people together in Solomon's Colonnade at the Temple. While you need organization in your home (think about when your extended family gathers for Thanksgiving or Christmas), it's definitely a more organic reality. Another more familiar way is saying that we want a Gathered expression of community life and Scattered reality.

TEMPLE	HOME
Organized	Organic
Gathered	Scattered

We have already seen that structure and spontaneity appear central to the experience of the early church.

TEMPLE	HOME
Organized	Organic
Gathered	Scattered
Structured	Spontaneous

But of course there are other words on this continuum. Perhaps you've read a book called *The Starfish and the Spider* that discusses some movemental properties. Or maybe you've read the gem of a book called *Recovering the Past*, which looks at how the Roman and the Celtic church came together in the Synod of Whitby in AD 664 and began to work in concert with each other, evangelizing the whole of Europe in just a few hundred years.

From a New Testament point of view, the beginning of the church immediately had **two** expressions of church life: Temple and Home. Again, it's important

TEMPLE	HOME
Organized	Organic
Gathered	Scattered
Structured	Spontaneous
Spider	Starfish
Roman	Celtic

that we understand that the word "home" or "household" is referring to a group of 20–70 people. Let's be careful not to drag our Western nuclear family lens into the scripture.

OIKOS IN OUR CONTEXT

If you're a church leader, it doesn't matter if you're from a mainline liturgical tradition or a free-flowing, attractional, non-denominational church. Rural, suburban, urban; Temple is what you know. It's probably the context in which you grew up. Maybe it's what you went to seminary to learn to lead. It's what you go to conferences about. It's simply what you know. And it is rare for me to meet a leader within a Western church who isn't already pretty good at this (and many are great at it). The Temple reality is something that we all understand.

What we need to understand, learn, and embrace if we are going to become leaders in a movement is the same thing that Paul had to learn—the *oikos* in the social space. It's the single most significant vehicle of mission that God has ever released on the world.

Ever.

Let's be quite clear: in the 270 years between Pentecost and the Edict of Milan, the millions brought into the Kingdom are principally won through the vehicle of the *oikos*.

I am not the only one saying this.

All of the evidence is vast compared to anything else. It tells us, unequivocally, that the evangelization of the known world at the time was through the Greco-Roman household.

This is what we are rediscovering in this new century as Generation Y comes onto the scene and opts not to deconstruct the rubble caused by the cultural earthquake anymore, but chooses to reconstruct instead. They pick up the remnants of what they find and say, "You know what? We could build with this!"

They want to reconnect with their parents, with their grandparents, with their aunts and uncles. It's happening all over the Western world, and it is symptomatic of a wider movement spreading. We see it as people are moving away from the deification of the nuclear family, represented in Christian circles by small groups, toward the release of extended family-sized groups on mission. *The* oikos *is being rediscovered.*

We must be very careful how the lens we use to understand the world colors what we see. Let me give you a practical example.

We know that there was a 50-year period when all missionaries were expelled from communist China. A steel curtain was dropped around the country. We know that there were about one million Christians when the curtain dropped. Five decades later, when restrictions were loosened and Christians began to venture into the country, they found something fascinating: The church had exploded. In that short period, the church had grown from one million to more than 60 million Christians.

How did the Chinese Christians do this?

They did it through something that became known as cell church. In other words, because public space worship was outlawed, these groups of Christians met in homes, secretly, to continue to be God's people on mission. After looking at this phenomenon, something fascinating happened. The Western church used this cell model as the birthplace for small group life by starting groups of six to 12 people. It was fascinating to see this happen in the 1980s.

But here is where our cultural lens colors our perspective: In China (and in Korea and Latin America as well), the role of the extended family remains central to Chinese cultural identity, even for their youth. Everything is built around and revolves around the extended family. So when the church in China grows that quickly in cells, it isn't cells of six to 12 people (the nuclear family size). It is groups of 20–40 people meeting in homes (the extended family size).

Similarly, the other two movements in "house church" in Korea (cell church) and South America (base communities) have been used and interpreted to inspire growth in the Western church. But again, extended household size groups were usually at the heart of these movements. But because a Western Christian sees "cell" or "house" in the title, they think nuclear family. And we end up with something quite different. The last 30 years of contemporary church life has been colored by this understanding of "cell". This led to the rise and slow decline of the small group movement.

Now again, I'm not saying there isn't a place for the "personal space" (six to 12 people). What I'm suggesting is that, sociologically speaking, in every culture on the face of the earth, that personal space group locates itself within a wider extended family. There is a place for smaller groups, but that place seems to be located best within something bigger in that social space realm.

Our cultural lens launched a movement within the church based on a misunderstanding of another culture.

How fascinating is that?!

I want to make sure we don't do the same thing as we read these passages in Acts.

I believe Missional Communities[50] are an expression of the social space on mission that we see in the New Testament. Why do I believe this is the Holy Spirit working to connect us to a vehicle of mission he used in the New Testament Church? Because I see it happening all over the world. Whether it us the United States, China, South America, Nepal, Africa or Scandinavia; *I see it everywhere.* If I've learned one thing over all my years in ministry, it's this: When you see something popping up all over the world, often disconnected from each other, it means the Holy Spirit is revealing something that he believes is important and wants to emphasize.

I am sometimes asked what I believe the future of Missional Communities is. My answer is that the Missional Community is merely the cocoon for something even more beautiful: *the extended family on mission.* Missional

....

[50] For a greater understanding of Missional Communities, read our book *Leading Missional Communities.*

Communities nurture and cultivate the important principles and life lessons that eventually manifest themselves in healthy extended families on Mission. Missional Community helps us get somewhere; it's a vehicle, not a destination. But a spiritual extended family—the *oikos*—is *the thing*—is *the destination*.

RELEARNING *OIKOS*

Think of it this way. If you're trying to learn or relearn something, you have to construct a context in which that learning can take place.

Here's an example. Just imagine for a moment everyone in the world forgot how to drive a car. People would have these hunks of metal on wheels in their driveways and not know what to do with them. One day, you would hear, "There was a time when they used to drive them, sit in them, and go places."

"No way!"

"Yeah! That circular thing is a wheel, and you can turn it, and it directs where that heavy thing would go. (By the way, it's called a car.)"

"Really? Because we've been using it for kids to climb on and we've put planters in the headlights. You mean it's not to be used as a lawn ornament?"

Imagine that world.

Your friend has told you this, and you do a little digging, and after a while, you find this book that talks about how to drive a car. What would you do? You wouldn't just get on the road and take the car out for a spin. You would have no idea what you were doing. You have no idea how people would react, or for that matter, how many people you might kill with that metal death trap. What you would do is get the car on a racetrack where you would have space to test out the car without hurting anyone. It would provide a space for you to experiment and get your bearings while driving this vehicle.

Now come back to our day, where we've lost the extended family and the *oikos* on mission.

What we are doing with Missional Communities (20–50 people acting as an extended family on mission together) is constructing an *oikos* that helps us understand what the New Testament church did and how they did family on mission. Missional Communities aren't the end goal. They are the vehicle that gets us back to the original thing. MCs[51] serve as the test track where we can get to know this foreign thing before we take it back into full service.

In 50 years, people will look back and say, "It's hilarious—they used to make people get in MCs because they didn't know how to do this. Isn't that amazing?"

PAUL AND *OIKOS*

But I'm getting slightly ahead of myself.

Let's return to scripture and ask this question: *How did Paul discover this same thing we've been discussing?*

Acts 8:1-3

> *On that day a great persecution broke out against the church in Jerusalem, and all except the apostles were scattered throughout Judea and Samaria. Godly men buried Stephen and mourned deeply for him. But Saul began to destroy the church. Going from house to house, he dragged off both men and women and put them in prison.*

This is fascinating. As we said before, Paul (Saul) targeted the household once the public space was taken away. So let's see if we can understand all that was happening here. Stephen had been stoned, but he had been stoned in such a way that breaks many of the Jewish rituals and laws for such a case. The ending of Acts 7 is a comedy of errors in how the religious rulers handled his sentencing and death. Seemingly realizing they had overstepped, they decided to go all the way.

Remember that the church for the first eight years was exclusively located in Jerusalem. You can see the enemy's plan: "They are all here in one place, like fish in a barrel. What I'll do is drop a grenade in that barrel and take them out in one fell swoop." And so Paul (Saul) was unleashed on the church, demolishing it one household at a time.

....

[51] We will use this abbreviation for Missional Communities hereafter.

Clearly, the apostles saw what was happening and decided a quick way forward: everyone needed to vacate the city, but they would stay in Jerusalem as the church's grounding point.[52] Perhaps it was to equip and instruct those scattered believers that James, the newly recognized leader of the church, wrote his now-canonized letter.

Look what happens in verse 4 of the same chapter as these early believers were all scattered: "Those who had been scattered preached the word wherever they went." It seems inconceivable to me, as these people left Jerusalem and went to other places in this first great scattering, that they didn't continue to travel with their *oikos*. If the majority of your life was lived with this group of 20–70 people, and if you understood your identity as a Christian was located within this family, that's who you would move with. It's not the atomized individual leaving the city—it's families leaving together and traveling as a pack to a new place.

Notice what happened when they scattered. The enemy's plan completely backfired. When disciples are scattered, they do what they are trained to do: Proclaim the Kingdom. Preach good news to the poor. Heal the sick. Make new disciples. Read the rest of Acts 8. That's what happened! The enemy's plan didn't work; in fact, it had the exact opposite effect, because of what the disciples did in the *oikos*.

And Paul saw that happening.

On his first missionary journey, Paul discovered a way of articulating the message in the context into which he was reaching. On his second journey, he discovered the methodology that would unleash a movement for centuries to come. What he saw in Jerusalem, he learned to use as he extended God's mission throughout the Roman Empire.

On the second missionary journey, Paul went without Barnabas. They had a falling out about Barney's cousin, John Mark. After John Mark had left them high and dry because of the dangers found in Galatia and ran home to his mother (literally), Barnabas wanted him back on the team. Paul would have nothing to do with it. It wasn't so much an issue of forgiveness as trust.

....

[52] Acts 8:1

Forgiveness is freely given, but trust is earned. Clearly, Paul didn't trust Mark.[53]

Barnabas and Mark went back to Cyprus, and Paul took Silas, one of the leaders in Jerusalem, with him. They walked north, through the Cilician Gates in the Taurus mountains. No doubt, Paul remembered all of the painful times of his hidden years spent in a cave in the very same mountains as they were walking toward Galatia. It appears Paul was trying to get to Ephesus. He was constantly trying to get to major centers of population, and Ephesus was one of the three most important cities in the whole of the Roman Empire.

But the Spirit stopped Paul from going south.

Then Paul thought, "Well, maybe I'll go north, to the beaches of the Black Sea and Bythinia." But the Spirit of Jesus prevented them from going that way as well.

If you can't go north, you can't go south, and you came from the east, that leaves only you one direction: west.

So Paul and Silas came to the terminus of the road in Troas, locally known as Alexandria because it was the place where Alexander the Great landed and from where he conducted his military campaign across Asia Minor. Troas was in many ways the gateway to Asia, and had many statues of Alexander

---

[53] Please see my book *Multiplying Missional Leaders* for a greater exploration of this.

adorning the city. There, Paul had a dream of a man from Macedonia, Alexander's home region in Greece.

I wonder what he looked like—the man in the dream. My guess? He looked like Alexander. Paul was in an eastern Asian city with one Greek face everywhere: Alexander. The man said to him, "Come over and help us!"

Timothy had already joined Paul and Silas in Lystra, and Luke had joined them in Troas. They hopped in a boat and crossed the Aegean Sea into the port city of Neapolis to make their way to the principal city of Macedonia. This city was named for the king who ruled the region—a king who happened to be Alexander's dad Philip. So the city was called Philippi. (All this naming cities after yourself does seem a bit narcissistic, doesn't it?)

INNOVATION AND *OIKOS*

Philippi had become a retirement community for former officers of the Roman army. They were given a small plot of land and invited to build a house there and were often given a small pension. So this was a community of wealth and of disposable income. *But it was also a community that didn't speak Greek. They spoke Latin.*

And we know from the scriptures and the archaeological record that this city had no synagogue. So what was Paul to do?

He had stepped into Europe for the first time. (I know I'm personally grateful for that!) But when he made this step, he entered a culture that was markedly different from any culture he had ever spent time trying to evangelize. There was no synagogue. He may not even speak the language.

So he thought to himself, "OK, there must be somebody in this city who has heard of the God of the scriptures. Otherwise, this is going to be a long, long job. Well, the ritual ablutions of the Jews require running water, and running water is found by rivers."

Paul knew that places that didn't have enough Jews to form a synagogue would often have gathering places for prayer by a river. So he asked around and someone pointed him to a spot outside the city walls. There he found a place of prayer where people who believed in the God of the scriptures gathered.

They were all women.

One of those women was someone who was involved in high fashion, like our modern *haute couture*.

Acts 16:13-15

> On the Sabbath we went outside the city gate to the river, where we
> expected to find a place of prayer. We sat down and began to speak
> to the women who had gathered there. **One of those listening
> was a woman from the city of Thyatira named Lydia, a dealer
> in purple cloth.** She was a worshiper of God. The Lord opened her
> heart to respond to Paul's message. When she and the members
> of her household were baptized, she invited us to her home. "If you
> consider me a believer in the Lord," she said, "come and stay at my
> house." **And she persuaded us.** (emphasis mine)

Lydia's house was populated with models—high-fashion models. That was the business she was in. People would come to her home, or she would visit the home of the nobility and bring her models to show the clothing she had available (purple cloth) for these high-rolling customers.

Paul and his team knew the Person of Peace strategy. We know they did because Luke is the writer not only of Acts but also of the book of Luke, where, in exact detail, he outlined Jesus' principal strategy for evangelism in Luke 9-10. It's the strategy of relationship building that Jesus gave first to the 12 and then to the 72, and it is the exact same strategy used over and over again by the early church and by Paul. We see it at work here.

When you find a Person of Peace, stay in his or her home (his or her *oikos*) and do not go from *oikos* to *oikos*.[54]

I don't know how something like the situation I am about to describe would be received in your culture. Imagine four young preachers turning up in your town and starting to evangelize in the high-fashion industry. Imagine the attractive young women asking these preachers to live with them. Maybe that would fly in Amsterdam, but I suspect in most places that's a no go!

Peter Wagner made a funny observation about this passage. He noted that four single men went to Phillipi, and only two left! Luke and Timothy stayed behind. I wonder why. Coincidence? I think not.[55]

Here's the thing: Paul was introduced to an entirely new mode of evangelism. His standard method was the public gathering at the synagogue. He usually went to large cities that had a good number of Jews. Archeology tells us that some of these synagogues were as large as our average-sized church buildings.

Paul usually began in the public space and allowed the message to permeate the social space. But with the public space of the synagogue removed, he had to find another way. Now he had *oikos* as his principal location of mission. Every day, Paul went to the public place of prayer and back to Lydia's home. He did this *every day*.

Every day, they created the rhythm of a public space gathering at the river, and every day they returned to Lydia's home and continued to operate on the continuum we have already covered.

....

[54] Luke 10:7

[55] See C. Peter Wagner's *The Book of Acts: A Commentary* for greater exploration of this.

UNLIKELY *OIKOS*

As they went every day, a young slave girl beset by a demon cried out. And for the life of me, I can't understand why our translations don't give us this information, but this is what it says in the original Greek: this girl is demonized by a *python* spirit.

Why is it not in there? I'm not sure.

Here is why it's helpful. The *python* spirit is clearly identified with the Oracle of Delphi. This oracle was a demonically inspired oracle that the leaders of the day would visit to discover the future. The spirit demonizing this girl, connected to the future-telling oracle, gave her something special that her masters capitalized on. She could tell people the future.

Acts 16:16. *Once when we were going to the place of prayer, we were met by a female slave who had a spirit by which she predicted the future. She earned a great deal of money for her owners by fortune-telling.*

She gained a lot of money for her masters.

Every day, she stood behind Paul and his men and yelled out to passersby, "Listen to these men! They know how you can be saved!"

In the presence of Jesus, the spirits cry out. They don't necessarily cry out what they want to cry out but they are compelled to speak nonetheless. Paul ignored it for as long as he could (which is my recommendation as well—ignore them for as long as possible). But eventually he just got tired of it, and commanded the spirit to be silent and to leave her. Understandably, her masters were furious. They had just lost a sizable amount of income.

They dragged Paul and Silas before the magistrates. Standing behind the magistrates (as we discussed before) were the *lictors* with their *fasces*, their great bundles of rods. In Macedonia, Philippi was known as "little Rome," so it was a place where Roman justice was executed effectively. The magistrates found Paul and Silas guilty and had them tied to a post and beaten. It's reasonable to think that Paul got a little extra abuse because, when they removed his clothes, they would have seen the scars of the many other beatings he had received before. To them, this would mean he was obviously a troublemaker.

The magistrates threw Paul and Silas into prison, which, according to local tradition, was in a cave. The chains that confined Paul and Silas were probably anchored into the back wall. This was where the worst prisoners were kept. Many of these prisons were fashioned so that the excrement would flow back to these places, providing the worst possible conditions for these hardened criminals.

So Paul and Silas were at the back of the cave doing what anyone would do—praising God. "About midnight Paul and Silas were praying and singing hymns to God, and the other prisoners were listening to them."[56]

Allow me to guess what I think might be happening here, with what is, perhaps, a little expository interlude. Paul and Silas's songs permeated the walls of the prison. The songs spread down the streets of Philippi. They rose above the rooftops and into the first heaven, where the creatures of the sky live. They ascended to the second heaven, where the angelic host is found. Into the third heaven, the songs of these prisoners continued to rise. In time, the praises came into the very throne room of the Lord Almighty. The Lord heard their worship—and he began to tap his foot.[57]

Acts 16:26-34

> Suddenly there was such a violent earthquake [God tapping his feet to the beat of their worship] that the foundations of the prison were shaken. At once all the prison doors flew open, and everyone's chains came loose. The jailer woke up, and when he saw the prison doors open, he drew his sword and was about to kill himself because he thought the prisoners had escaped. But Paul shouted, "Don't harm yourself! We are all here!"
>
> The jailer called for lights, rushed in and fell trembling before Paul and Silas. He then brought them out and asked, "Sirs, what must I do to be saved?"

[Remember what the slave girl had cried out?]

> They replied, "Believe in the Lord Jesus, and you will be saved—

....

[56] Acts 16:25

[57] I hope you will allow this rather exotic interpretation. Perhaps it's the inner preacher in me trying to get out.

*you and your household [referencing oikos]." Then they spoke the
word of the Lord to him and to all the others in his house. At that
hour of the night the jailer took them and washed their wounds;
then immediately he and all his household [referencing oikos] were
baptized. The jailer brought them into his house and set a meal
before them; he was filled with joy because he had come to believe
in God—he and his whole household [referencing oikos].*

Make no mistake. Paul saw how God was working here. He had an *oikos*,
which was the first church led by a woman. The next one is the first church led
by Anglicans—because all the children got baptized as well. (Sorry—that's a
little inside-the-family Anglican humor. I couldn't resist.)

The next day the magistrates found out that Paul was a Roman citizen.
Understandably, they tried to keep this quiet, because they had abused his
rights as a Roman. But there was no chance Paul was going to let that happen.
He asked that they be escorted from the city with official honors.

OIKOS IN CORINTH

Paul went on to have all sorts of adventures in Macedonia. They went to
Berea, where the good-hearted people came to Christ in scores. It seems
that an entire synagogue came to faith. He went to Athens, which we've

already loosely covered, and then went on to Corinth, right in the middle of an important time in the history of this city. Thousands of Jews were living in a refugee camp because Caesar Claudius had expelled all the Jews from Rome.[58]

Apparently, there was a riot having to do with Crestus (referencing "the Christ") among the Jews in Rome. Romans were congenitally afraid of urban unrest, and Claudius wanted nothing to do with it. So he exiled all the Jews from Rome. He threw them all out, including the highborn Jewish nobility like Priscilla and Aquila.

These Roman Jews had to find somewhere else to go, and the obvious place was the second largest city in the Roman Empire, one that in many ways resembled Rome itself—Corinth.

It's interesting, from a geography standpoint. Two cities, Corinth and Cenchreae, were separated by nine miles and an isthmus of land that connected Achaia and the Peloponnesian peninsula, which was the ancient home of Sparta. A ship would come into Cenchreae, unload its goods, get picked up and put onto rollers (literally), and pushed for nine miles to Corinth on dry land. There the ship would be put back into the water. (Clearly, this was

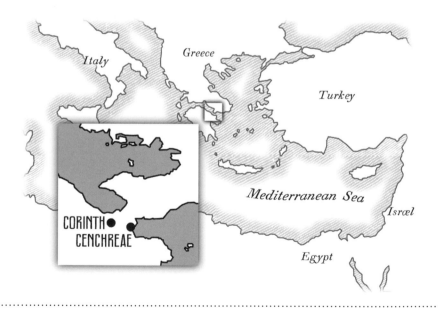

---

[58] It says this in the text of Acts, and it is supported by the historian Suetonius.

before someone had the wonderful idea of *canals*.)

It's just an incredible thing to think about.

In the midst of this, there was probably a large refugee camp. And if you have many refugees, what profession is pretty lucrative?

Tent-making.

Acts 18:1-3

> After this, Paul left Athens and went to Corinth. There he met a Jew named Aquila, a native of Pontus, who had recently come from Italy with his wife Priscilla, because Claudius had ordered all Jews to leave Rome. Paul went to see them, and because he was a tentmaker as they were, he stayed and worked with them.

Paul joined Aquila and Priscilla's *oikos*. As we've said, the *oikos* (the household of 20–70 blood and non-blood people) was the center of Greco-Roman life. It was the center of social life including education, healing, nurture and commerce.

Paul understood that if he functioned in the *oikos*, it was a place of stability (where it was difficult to persecute people, particularly if it was located in the household of the nobility) and a place where community could grow. Thus, the *oikos* was an absolute genius vehicle for mission. Do you see that?

Rodney Stark, in his brilliant book *The Rise of Christianity*, describes the effect of the *oikos* this way:

> Christianity revitalized life in Greco-Roman cities by providing new norms and new kinds of social relationships able to cope with urgent urban problems. To cities filled with the homeless and impoverished, Christianity offered charity as well as hope. To cities filled with newcomers and strangers, Christianity offered an immediate basis for attachments. To cities filled with orphans and widows, Christianity provided a new and expanded sense of family. To cities

---

[59] Rodney Stark has written several outstanding books, the one mentioned above, *The Rise of Christianity*, as well as *The Triumph of Christianity*.

torn by violent ethnic strife, Christianity offered a new basis for social solidarity. And to cities faced with epidemics, fires, and earthquakes, Christianity offered effective nursing services.[59]

METHOD:
The most reproducible Kingdom process that results in the most significant Kingdom progress.

This wasn't happening in huge settings. This was happening in extended families of 20–70 people. Paul had finally found the method and the vehicle that would win the day.

From this moment on, whenever Paul mentioned Priscilla and Aquila in his greetings, he always said, "And make sure to greet the church that meets in their *oikos.*" Every time.[60] Why? He had such fond memories. That was the way he remembered them.

It was here that it all came together for him. It started with the first woman he came into contact with in Europe: Lydia. It ended with the most significant house he encountered in his second missionary journey: the household of Priscilla and Aquila.

Of course, in Corinth Paul faced the normal difficulties. The synagogue rejected him, and so he moved *right next door* (what an amazing character!) to the *oikos* of Titius Justus, a worshiper of God.

OIKOS METHODOLOGY

One more point.

Imagine the scene. Paul was meeting the Ephesian church elders (each a head of an *oikos*) at the beach at Miletus. Paul had completed his three missionary journeys. In his first missionary journey, he discovered how to shape the message of the gospel to the context in which he found himself. In his second missionary journey, he engaged with, specifically, the New Testament missionary vehicle of the *oikos*. And by his third missionary journey, he was able to say to the Ephesian elders, "You know my ministry. You know that I

----

[60] For example, in Romans 16:3.

have not kept anything back or held back from sharing anything that would be helpful. You know the continuum of life from which I have operated."

Consider what it says in Acts 20:20: "You know that I have not hesitated to preach anything that would be helpful to you but have taught you **publicly** and from **house to house**." (*oikos* to *oikos*)

What seems clear to me is that when Lydia came to faith, then her family, then the Philippian jailer and his family, when Priscilla and Aquila joined him in his work (all this during his second missionary journey), Paul saw something, and it changed his method for spreading the gospel.

Now, was Paul illustrative or catalytic?

In other words, did this method exist before Paul and he simply illustrated it, or did Paul discover something that catalyzed the way the church would function for centuries to come? Honestly, I'm not sure. And I'm not sure historians are either. It's a fascinating question, but it's not the most important takeaway.

What I do know is that the methodology of *oikos* traces all the way through the book of Acts and through the early church and straight through to the evangelization of Europe, Africa, Asia, and beyond. Whenever the church can gather publicly, it does. But it never forsakes the primary missional vehicle of the *oikos*. By living on this continuum, using this method, a persecuted people changed the world forever.

10

∾ PAUL: ∾
MIRACULOUS + MOVEMENT

As we will explore in this chapter, all of this came to a head in Ephesus. We've seen several times where Paul regularly set his sights for Ephesus, knowing what an important part it played in the Roman Empire. He was looking for a massive breakthrough to happen, looking to establish a beachhead for the whole of eastern Asia and beyond.

MIRACULOUS:
The recognizable demonstration of a Kingdom invasion.

So we have a Mission. We have a Message. We have a Method. But we also need the Miraculous to be truly Movemental.

Think of it this way: if you can do the work of the Kingdom without the Holy Spirit's active involvement, you aren't really doing the work of the Kingdom.

I would suggest to you that the scriptures are a clear testimony to that. Paul, as he went about his first and second missionary journeys, obviously operated in the power of the Holy Spirit. But in his third missionary journey, he embraced a kind of understanding that was quite different than his previous journeys. It took him from being just a man with a mission to a man with a movement.

Certainly, Paul had operated in the power of God before, but it seems that he did so in a new way in Ephesus.

In 2 Corinthians 12, Paul gives us a picture of what happened between his second and third missionary journeys. (Ephesus is where he ends up in his third journey.) At the end of his second journey, Paul took a vow and shaved off all the hair on his body. My take on this particular part of Paul's life is that he took a Nazarite vow.[61]

With this particular vow, you shave off all the hair on your body and put the hair in a bag. (It all seems very weird, I know.) Paul's plan was to take the bag by hand to the Temple. He would give it to the priest to place on the flames of the altar. And in view of God's mercy, he would give himself like a living sacrifice.[62]

The second journey ended as Paul left Priscilla and Aquila and eventually made his way to Jerusalem. Do you know what he had with him? His bag of hair. (Still gross, I know.) He gave it to the priest because the point of the vow was that you make a special request to God or ask God to give you an answer to something.

Now this is an educated guess, but I think this was Paul's request: "God, would you get rid of these blasted Judaizers—these pains in my neck? They are going behind all the churches we have planted spreading heresy and thrashing these new churches to bits."

The Biblical phrase for what I termed "pain in the neck" is the "thorn in my flesh."

In Numbers 23, the "thorns in the flesh" were the Canaanites if Israel didn't get rid of them. In Ezekiel, they were the people around you who continue to trouble you. In other words, in the Bible, "thorn in the flesh" usually means *people*.

My suspicion is that Paul's "thorn in the flesh" were the Judaizers following him wherever he started Kingdom work. So I believe that he asked the Lord, "Remove this troubling influence in my life that is killing the churches I'm planting!"

The Lord said no.

Maybe Paul continued: "What I mean, Lord, in case you didn't understand the

----

[61] 2 Corinthians 12:1-10, Acts 18:18

[62] Perhaps this is what Paul had in mind when he later wrote from Corinth at the end of his third missionary journey to the Romans: *Therefore, I urge you, brothers and sisters, in view of God's mercy, to offer your bodies as a living sacrifice, holy and pleasing to God—this is your true and proper worship.*

first time—all of those people who are ruining the proclamation of grace in the gospel because they want people to become Jews first before coming to faith in your son Jesus. Could you, you know, get rid of them?"

God said, "Hmmmm. No."

Perhaps empowered by the fact that, in his Gethsemane moment, Jesus went three times to the Father asking if there was another way, Paul asked a third time: "Lord, I mean it. I don't know what to do. Every time I plant a church, I worry I'm going to turn around and these guys are going to pop up like wolves and devour the sheep. I'm serious about this. I'll even make a vow this third time. Please answer my request!"

And the Lord said, "No."

"My grace," the Father said, "is sufficient for you. For my power is made perfect in your weakness." That led Paul to say, "Therefore I shall boast even more in my weakness. My struggles. My trials. My persecutions."

My guess is this was a fresh moment of surrender for Paul. It's not that he hadn't surrendered before, but this was at a new and deeper level. Paul embraced the tentmaker work. He embraced the Judaizers. He embraced the role of an Apostle who is unseen.

This is what the scriptures say about Paul's time in Ephesus: "God did **extraordinary** miracles through Paul so that even handkerchiefs and aprons that had touched him were taken to the sick, and their illnesses were cured and the evil spirits left them."[63]

This is the only time in all of the scriptures that the word "extraordinary" is used with the word "miracle." Usually a miracle is considered extraordinary enough without this adjective. But in this case, the things Paul was doing were so above and beyond what Luke might think of with miracles that they called for the qualifying term *extraordinary* in the book of Acts.

Here's what could have been happening: Paul was unable to visit the sick because he was working. He had a full-time job. So he said, "Look, I'm kind

....

[63] Acts 19:11-12

of in the middle of making this tent. I've got to finish it, and I don't have time to step away for an hour. But so that your friend knows that I'm praying for them as I work, take this sweat band to him."

So they took the sweatband and went to the sick person.

"Paul's praying for you *right now*. He couldn't come, but here's his sweat band."

That person was healed. Delivered. Transformed. *And Paul wasn't even there!*

All tentmakers wore thick leather aprons so that they didn't pierce their skin with the sharp needles they used. Paul would say, "Here, take this apron, lay it on her, and tell her I'm praying for her."

Healed.

It was amazing. People were astonished. Then the revival really got going when a deliverance went off the deep end with the seven sons of Sceva a few verses later.

Acts 19:13-18

> Some Jews who went around driving out evil spirits tried to invoke the name of the Lord Jesus over those who were demon-possessed. They would say, "In the name of the Jesus whom Paul preaches, I command you to come out." Seven sons of Sceva, a Jewish chief priest, were doing this. One day the evil spirit answered them, "Jesus I know, and Paul I know about, but who are you?" Then the man who had the evil spirit jumped on them and overpowered them all. He gave them such a beating that they ran out of the house naked and bleeding.

When this became known to the Jews and Greeks living in Ephesus, they were all seized with fear, and the name of the Lord Jesus was held in high honor. Many of those who believed now came and openly confessed what they had done.

These seven men were priests with their dad. All it took was seven naked vicars running around the streets of Ephesus for revival to break out!

I don't know how God will do it in your work. I don't know how God will do it through your family, community, and mission. But I believe the miraculous will happen if you depend on the miraculous power of God, embrace your weakness, and say, "The cracks of my life are the places where the power of God is able to seep through."

One of the people who proved hugely influential in my life put it this way:

> When you tell people that you believe Jesus was raised from the dead, it's natural for them to say, "Prove it." And to be honest, who wouldn't ask that? The fact of the matter is we probably are going to have a difficult time arguing the facts about Jesus' resurrection. But if Paul was right, "The same spirit that raised Christ Jesus from the dead is now alive in me," we can prove it. There is resurrection happening in our life every day. In our hearts, but also in our physical world. I regularly see miracles happen, and when people see that, I can say, "Look, the resurrection is still happening!" That's something that has far more power than arguing with people.[64]

I've thought about this a lot. Why would God continually say no to Paul? After all, this wasn't something selfish Paul was asking for. He'd grown quite close with the people in the various churches he'd planted, and they were being emotionally and spiritually terrorized by these religious zealots. He was acting as a good shepherd, looking after his flock.

Here's what I think it is: God wanted Paul to be perfectly clear that any lasting success he achieved has nothing to do with him. He must act as an agent of the Kingdom in such a way that coming and going, he left this new church plant in the hands of God, knowing that he had no control.

Just think about Paul for a second.

Doesn't he seem like he'd be a bit of a control freak?

What God is putting back on Paul is the act of *submission*. "Will you submit to my ways, my process, my Kingdom, even if 'success' is always shaky and uncertain?"

....

[64] A summation of some of the ideas from John Wimber's classic book *Power Evangelism*

You see, the temptation for Paul was to think he was gifted enough, smart enough, strong willed enough to accomplish the things of the Kingdom. This man was a force of a nature, and you get the sense reading some of his letters that he was slightly aware of his own leanings toward arrogance.

But he submitted, and in many ways, it was a deeper revelation of God's mission into which Paul was merging.

And what did this kind of submission do?

It unlocked untold Kingdom breakthrough as the Holy Spirit went to work through Paul.

SUSTAINABLE AND SCALABLE

MOVEMENT:
When individual experience is mobilized into communal expression resulting in a groundswell of exponential breakthrough.

Movemental change will come only if we have something that is sustainable and scalable. By sustainable, I mean that something continues beyond the period of time of the breakthrough we last saw. Movements require things to be sustained longer. And often a rhythmic pattern needs to be embraced.

One of the fundamental components of sustainability is *scalability*. Here's what I mean: if our methodology requires leaders and events with endless amounts of training and endless amounts of energy, resources, and money (something where only the real elite get to participate), then we're done.

We just are.

The sustainability of something is 100 percent dependent on us scaling it from the smallest size community to the largest so that it can grow and multiply and spread. *Our vehicles must be reproducible.* And what we do in the micro must be represented in what we do in the macro.

Many people think that something like *revival* is like a giant aerosol can God is waving in the sky, and when he sprays, it's going to change everything. And that's not what is going to happen. It's just not. Yet for most of my adult life, that's the expectation I have encountered in the church.

In England, I have seen revival taking place for at least 40 years—*and it has been wasted*.

In my lifetime in England, I have seen all of the markers that church historians would say are the mileposts of either the word "revival" or the word "awakening." There is absolutely no distinction between what I've seen and these other periods of history. The only difference is that we have not created sustainable and scalable models. And I would suggest this is because of our propensity toward individualism and self-indulgence.

We would much prefer the event to be the answer rather than the process. We would much prefer the conference with the amazing leader to be the key trigger instead of our life being the crucible of transformation as we invest our life in another person, who invests his or her life in another, who does the same, and on and on.

So we, like children in a storm, are blown from this thing to that, hoping that God will spray the magic aerosol can that will change everything, rather than creating sustainable and scalable models for the Holy Spirit to work through movementally.

Massive conferences with amazing, charismatic leaders aren't sustainable or scalable.[65] History has shown us this time and time again. On the other hand, having people who know how to invest their lives in others, people who disciple others to disciple others, and who create lightweight and low maintenance vehicles for discipleship and mission have *always* been the principal way the Holy Spirit has created movemental change.

If it's going to be movemental, it needs to be scalable and sustainable.

So why do we constantly look for the next new shiny thing? One day, some mature leader somewhere is going to say, "You know what? We're not going to do that anymore. It's not scalable or sustainable, so I'm not doing it."

....

[65] Some faith traditions use words like "anointed" to describe these kinds of people.

That's what we see with Paul. He stumbled into something in the *oikos* that grabbed his heart and his mind, and you can almost see the wheels in his head turn as he thought, "I think we've got something here, guys. There's something going on here. Look how easy it multiplies. Look how well it does mission and discipleship. We've got to tinker with this thing and train others to do it."

In the early 1990s, right after one of our Missional Communities gave birth to another, I remember clear as day walking into the kitchen and saying to Sally, "I've seen it. That thing just multiplied. This is AMAZING. I honestly think this thing could change the world."

Why? Because it was scalable and sustainable. Normal people with 9-to-5 jobs had something they could take ownership of, something they could lead, grow, and multiply. They could be the ones taking new territory for the Kingdom. We weren't just seeing the Priesthood of all Believers but the Missionhood of all Believers. Once you've learned what it takes to give birth to one, that's all you need. You can teach others to do the same thing. You can learn from the little tree bearing lots of fruit.

That's what Paul sensed here.

Operate in the public space when you can, but use the social space as the principal place for mission. It's not that other space can't do it; it's just that it seems to be done best in this extended family size.

BECOMING MOVEMENTAL

By the time Paul got to Ephesus, he was going to function only from *oikos*. He functioned only in his tent-making *oikos*. He told the Ephesian elders, "You know how I have lived every day I've been with you. These hands of mine have supplied my needs and the needs of my team."[66]

He didn't look for gifts from churches to release him to preach as he did in Corinth. He didn't looking for an opportunity to build the church in the

---

[66] Acts 20:34

synagogue as he did in other places. Certainly, he gave the ancient people of God the first opportunity, as he always did, but in Ephesus they were obstinate and publicly maligned The Way.

So he left the Jews, taking his disciples with him, and rented the Hall of Tyrannus. Many New Testament scholars point to a scribe from the early church who made a margin note of what was happening here, as he carried on the memory of the church. Paul rented the Hall of Tyrannus during the siesta hours between midday and four in the afternoon.

Why? Because he had a job like everyone else!

He started work at sunrise, closed the shop at noon because of the heat of the day, and then reopened the shop at four when the cool of the evening made it easier to work. The workers continued until it was too dark to continue. In rural areas, workers might last only a few more hours, while in urban places, where they'd devised ways of illuminating the city, it would last a little longer.

So Paul, the tentmaker, was now building a movement in his spare time.

In finding the time in the middle of the day, Paul created a space of investment with his disciples. He held discussions daily in this lecture hall. I imagine this was very similar to watching the Apostles in Acts 2. This lecture hall was a very large space where Paul would invest in these men and allow others to listen in on what they were discussing and teasing out.[67] As a matter of fact, this was very similar to what Jesus' disciples experienced in the Sermon on the Mount. Remember, that passage starts with Matthew saying that all of these teachings were happening as a discussion with his disciples while the crowds listened in.[68]

Nothing was on television during these siesta hours in Ephesus, and thus, you would take your packed lunch and go hear Paul and his disciples hash it out. Sounds great. I imagine there was some worship in there too. You can imagine the conversations: "Hey, all the pubs are closed. Why don't we go listen in on Paul and his boys?"

....

[67] Acts 19:9-10
[68] Matthew 5:1-2

INFORMATION, IMITATION, INNOVATION

Let's pause here and understand where Paul was in his own personal journey.

He was now around 50 years old. At 30, he met Jesus on the road to Damascus. He spent three years in the Arabian desert, probably alone, spent 15 days with the Apostles in Jerusalem, and then disappeared for 10 years where he experienced rejection, failure, systematic torture, and excommunication.

Barnabas found him, and seven years later, Paul had two unbelievably successful missionary journeys and had planted many churches. But let's not forget that these were not easy times. There were still beatings, near-death escapes, exposure to the elements, and near starvation. It wasn't all champagne and roses.

Now Paul found himself in Ephesus at age 50, more than likely with the body of a 90-year-old man—and a sick one at that. He was staring mortality in the face and he had to be thinking that he wasn't going to last much longer. Either chronic injuries would take him, or he would have some fateful mishap with a Jewish synagogue or Roman magistrate.

"Will this thing outlast me?" Paul had to be wondering.

"I've planted some churches, but in the grand scheme of things, that's just a drop in the bucket of the Roman Empire. And honestly? It's just me out here with a few team members helping me. There has to be a better way." What would happen if he multiplied himself? What if it wasn't Paul who planted the churches? What if he trained people to do what he'd done so that they could do the same? And what if they went and did the same thing?"

And that's exactly what Paul did.

Extra-Biblical sources suggest that Paul had six disciples meeting with him in the Hall of Tyrannus: Timothy from Lystra, Gaius from Derbe, Aristarchus and Secundus from Thessalonica, Titus from Antioch, and Sopater from Berea. There also seems to be reason to think Silas and Epaphras were in and out of Ephesus during this time, though probably serving in a different capacity. It's worth noting, when you examine the list of these men, that the places they are from are the places where Paul had planted churches during his first two journeys.

These men represented the fruit of Paul's labor.

What we discover is that Paul didn't plant any of the other churches in the cities of eastern Asia that came under the sound of the gospel. Instead, these men he had trained did. The significant and important churches John wrote to in his Revelation? Other than Ephesus, it would appear all were planted by the men in whom Paul had invested—not Paul himself.

Some of these places went on to become missional sending centers themselves because Paul had taught them how to do this.

What Paul did was unleash a multipliable movement on the Roman world, taking all that he had learned and poured into those eight men, believing that those men would do greater things than he. This was just as Jesus had believed about his own disciples.

MISSIONAL SENDING CENTERS:
Communities that have enough spiritual mass, with leaders who embody the character and competency of Jesus, that they become places for reproducing, training, and sending leaders into the missional frontier, as well as a safe place of orbit for those leaders returning from the missional frontier.

Paul was aiming for a movement. He didn't want to rely on growth by addition. He wanted growth by multiplication. Time was too short. There had to be a better way. And finally, he found one.

Later, having assigned Timothy the task of leading the Ephesian church, he emphasizes this principle by reminding him in his second letter of this multiplying principle.[69] He was essentially saying, "Be sure to pass what you learned to the people who can multiply your investment."

In his time with these men, we see Paul working out the discipleship process of Information, Imitation, and Innovation. Paul gave the Information using the Socratic and Rabbinical method of statement, question, answer. Statement, question, answer.

....

[69] 2 Timothy 2:2: "And the things you have heard me say in the presence of many witnesses entrust to reliable people who will also be qualified to teach others."

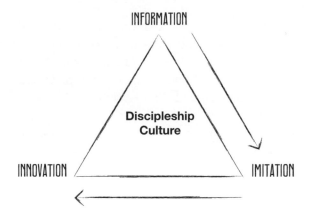

INFORMATION

Discipleship
Culture

INNOVATION   IMITATION

He used Imitation by pointing to his life and the way that he had learned to do things. Can you imagine a scenario where Paul didn't share what he had learned from his hidden years and his first two missionary journeys with his disciples? Don't you think he taught them to do the things he'd learned how to do? Can't you imagine him saying, "Guys, you're going to make mistakes along the way, but please, just make different ones! I've got the scars to show you what not to do most of the time."

While Paul was in Ephesus, a report came from Sosthenes about all that was happening in Corinth. If you remember, he was the former synagogue leader in Corinth and was beaten black and blue when his scheme against Paul turned on him in front of Governor Gallio.[70] Somewhere along the way, Sosthenes actually became a Christian and was one of the key leaders in the church in Corinth. He told Paul all that was happening in Corinth, and let's just say the news wasn't good.

There were, perhaps, four Corinthian letters, and we have two of them. You'll remember that Paul wrote 1 Corinthians from Ephesus to the Christians in Corinth, probably with Sosthenes by his side. While Paul was in Ephesus writing the Corinthians this canonical first letter, he asked them to reflect on his pattern of life, which was the same pattern he was living out in Ephesus.

. . . .

[70] Acts 18:14-17

GUARDIANS AND PARENTS

1 Corinthians 4:14-17

> *I am writing this not to shame you but to warn you as my dear children. Even if you had ten thousand guardians in Christ, you do not have many fathers, for in Christ Jesus I became your father through the gospel. Therefore I urge you to imitate me. For this reason I have sent to you Timothy, my son whom I love, who is faithful in the Lord. He will remind you of my way of life in Christ Jesus, which agrees with what I teach everywhere in every church.*

That word "guardians" is the Greek word *pedagogos*. It refers to a specific person who was hired by the parents and brought into the extended family *oikos* to stay with the family from the time the child was weaned until the age of 12 or 13. This guardian would teach the child the classical Greek education of reading, writing, arithmetic, and logic. The guardian was there to provide the basic information.

Now some people have mistakenly or unhelpfully suggested in many a sermon that you don't need these pedagogues. That's ludicrous. You need the *pedagogos* (the pedagogue). You need the basic information. But of course, you don't need that basic phase forever. At some point, you need more.

In this passage, Paul was referring to a pattern of life that everyone understood. He was shaping his message to a context so that people could comprehend it.

What you see in reading the New Testament is that the word "disciple" disappears after Acts 21 and isn't mentioned in Paul's or Peter's or John's letters.

Why? When the call to "make disciples" are the last words of Jesus, why would it drop off the pages of scripture so early on? How can this be? To me, this seems to be an important question.

The reason is that the gospel was moving away from the cultural heartland in the geographical area known as the Holy Land. The gospel was moving from Israel—from Jerusalem, Judea, and Samaria—and was now reaching the ends of the earth. In Corinth, there were very few (if any) rabbis and disciples. So, the vast majority of the pagan cities such as Corinth, Ephesus and Rome had no understanding of what the word "disciple" meant because that word was always used in reference to a rabbi.

These people had *no idea* what a rabbi was.

So Paul looked for an analogue, a guiding picture, that the church could understand, one that included all that was involved in discipleship to a rabbi. If you are being discipled by a rabbi, you certainly want to know what the rabbi knows. But a more important question is this: "How can I become who the rabbi is? Yes, I want to know what he knows, but I also want to be like him!"

Paul understood this relational context because he himself was a disciple of Gamaliel. Paul understood the world of rabbis and disciples, but suddenly he was on mission to people who didn't have a cultural reference point for it. I think he decided, "It's silly for me to try to explain this. There must be some cultural reference that I can use that gets to the heart of the discipleship process. They've got to get what spiritual formation looks like."

What metaphor did he use? The parent and the child.

Paul didn't use this metaphor in a paternalistic sense, but in the sense of formation, growth, and development. He said, "All of you have seen this picture. It's something you understand. As you are raised, there is a pedagogue who gives you the necessary information. It will be the foundation for all training later in life, but the parent offers the model to be imitated."

When the child turned 12, he or she went through a ritual, a moment of religious significance in the Greco-Roman *oikos*. The pedagogue brought a 12-year-old girl to her mother. Her mother, even though she lived with this appalling perspective of being a second-rate citizen outside the home, actually carried the most significant role inside it. She managed the whole household. Her role was to understand the complexity of the organic and organization components of the *oikos*. She knew how to deal with the sick. She oversaw the educational process. She managed the economic infrastructure and cash flow. She was the business manager and the shaper of a hospitable environment for guests. (Remember, pretty much all business was run through the home, and she oversaw this aspect of the business.) Make no mistake: this was a job. In fact, it was probably a job for three or four people.

From that point on, the girl "stood at the shoulder" of her mother, discovering how all the information she had learned was actually grounded in everyday life. Once she married, she would either *extend the oikos* or, along with her husband, *start a new oikos*.[71]

A son at the age of 12 was brought, in a similar ceremony, to the shoulder of his father to learn the trade of the family. He would learn to ask, "What is it that this family produces? " He would come to understand the trade, craft, or business of the house. Paul's father was a tentmaker. How do we know that? Because Paul was a tentmaker.

"What are you going to do when you grow up?" is an entirely new question of the last 100 years. Nobody ever asked that question of children previously. It would be ridiculous. Children were going to do what their parents did. It took such a rare set of circumstances for a son to do something else that the thought of asking the question would never have entered his mind.

From age 12 on, the son learned to imitate his father with the normal methods of apprenticeship in the craft and trade of the house.

This was the perfect metaphor for Paul, and thus, for the rest of the New Testament, the scriptures replace the rabbi/disciple relationship with the parent/child relationship. Look at the rest of the New Testament, and in almost every book, you will see that the way the text understands spiritual formation is through the lens of parent and child.

EPICENTER IN EPHESUS

This is what Paul did in Ephesus. As he formed his team with information and imitation, he sent them out. Colossians 1:7 puts it this way: "You learned it from Epaphras, our dear fellow servant, who is a faithful minister of Christ on our behalf, and who also told us of your love in the Spirit."

Paul had never met the church at Colossae. He had sent out Epaphras, and he represented all he had learned from Paul. Make no mistake.

....

[71] I cannot recommend Kenneth Bailey's book *Paul through Mediterranean Eyes* highly enough when it comes to understanding all of the culture and context at work in the book of 1 Corinthians.

Timothy and Titus carried letters and were sent out to plant churches. Paul was confident in sending them out because they had been shaped by the information, and they had imitated Paul and learned from his life. It's no surprise that they Innovated in these new contexts.

It's not like there was a telephone, and they could pick up the phone, call Paul, and ask, "Hey, what do you think I should do here?" No, they were thinking, "OK, I've spent a lot of time with Paul. When I see him, I can see Jesus at work. It's helpful to have a flesh-and-blood example. *If Paul were here, what do I think he would do?"*

Paul had enacted what I discussed in my book *Multiplying Missional Leaders*: he had developed a leadership pipeline that was sustainable and could be repeated over and over and over again with these eight men as they planted churches and returned. It happened as they went on short pastoral trips and returned. They took letters, settled disputes, shepherded communities through difficult times, and returned. It was training, deployment, and review time and time again in this two-year period (and beyond).

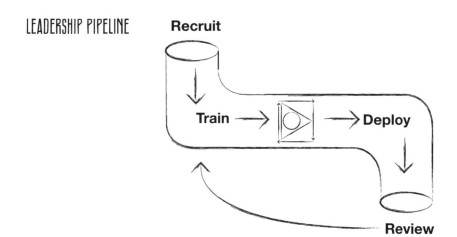

In living out this pattern for several years myself, I've noticed something interesting at play. As I delegate and release people and then review with them, it helps me recognize how far they've come. But it also helps give me a sense of how God might want to use them in the future. Usually I'll see something, sit on it and observe a bit longer, and ask the Lord for discernment on it. And as we keep reviewing, something starts to emerge that I'm able to share with them as I see the Lord working through them and in them.

Back to the story. What Paul had done was create an epicenter for a movement.

When you look at it, Paul's effect in that city and that region was amazing. When you see the description in Acts 19 of all the Lord did through Paul, it's clear that the Lord did such work that not only did all of the Gentiles hear the gospel, but so did all the Jews. "This went on for two years, so that all the Jews and Greeks who lived in the province of Asia heard the word of the Lord."[72]

Understand this very clearly: Ephesus was the most important church in the world for the next 400 years. It became the epicenter of almost everything. It was enormously significant. And this church that became the center of a worldwide movement was one that Paul planted in his spare time.

Never think that God is unable to work through the restrictions of your life.

I fundamentally believe that if you embrace the mission of God, learn to share the message of the gospel in any context, and learn a scalable and sustainable methodology while embracing the miraculous, you will see a movement spread. People may not even remember you, but who cares about that? By the time we get to heaven and are welcomed at the gates, we'll be able to look around and see many who have come because of us.

We will be able to look around *in this lifetime* and see heaven come to earth right here and right now. We will see the chains of injustice loosed. We will see the captives delivered. We will see justice come to bear. We will see the sick made well. We will see the people come into the right relationship with their Father in heaven.

We will be people who step into a movement of God that has been unfolding before us for hundreds and thousands of years.

....

[72] Acts 19:10

11

∾ NAVIGATING ∾
THE SPIRITUAL TERRAIN

Before we move on to some of the essential mechanics of a movement in Part 4, let me share a few thoughts about navigating the spiritual terrain that comes with being this kind of leader.

The process of becoming the kind of leader who leads this type of movemental community is not quick or easy, as we've already seen in the life of Paul.

God is doing work in your life day-by-day, season-by-season, taking you through a process that shapes you into this kind of person. *The Holy Spirit is already at work in your life doing this*, but this is a never-ending process, isn't it?

There will be days when you sense his work, his presence, his blessing, and his grace as if it were the Second Coming. And, as you know, there will also be days where it feels like the opposite is true. We need to take only a fleeting glance at Paul's story to see this at work.

Perhaps the worst thing I could communicate in this book is that the process happening in you as a leader is quick or easy.

That's why it is so important to understand how to navigate this kind of terrain. When Barnabas found Paul in the cave, he was 43 years old. By the time Paul was 52, Ephesus had turned into a missional sending center, and the known world would never be the same again. *How was Paul able to attend to what God was doing in his heart to such a degree that all this was possible, despite what was swirling around him on any given day?*

Perhaps this picture can help us understand.

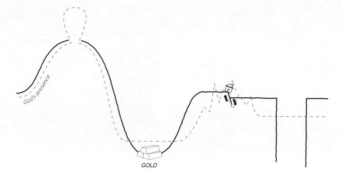

GOLD

Think of your life as a landscape. The landscape of our lives has high points and low points. There are places of great wonder and glory. And there are other places where we are clearly struggling. If we look at our lives in relation to the presence of God, then we have to say that, from a theological point of view, the Holy Spirit has already filled our lives. So we're asking him to take the presence that is within us and give us greater access to where that presence is and what that presence means.

It's not as though the Lord, in any genuine theological sense, leaves us. The Psalmist says, "Take not your Holy Spirit from us," but that's of course an Old Testament reality. From the point of the view of the Holy Spirit in the New Testament, we are baptized into a new life, we are regenerated by the Holy Spirit, and he will refill us. But he doesn't fill from the outside when we become a Christian. He fills us from the inside.

We often use the baptism language, so it seems as though he's coming from the outside, but we have to remember that once we've been made new, his presence is within us. Jesus describes how, from within us, a bubbling spring will overflow from time to time.

ERUPTION

We all have these eruptive moments of God's presence. We have incredible experiences where there seems to be an explosion of God's presence within us.[73] Maybe it happens in a time of prayer as happened in the life of Jesus.

....

[73] A few examples from the New Testament: Jesus with the Samaritan woman in John 4. Jesus with two disciples walking to Emmaus in Luke 24 ("Were our hearts not burning within us!?").

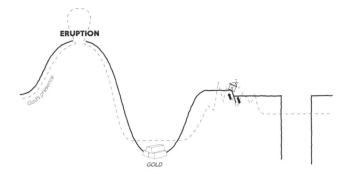

Maybe it happens in worship. Maybe you remember a time when you were a teenager at a camp or at a retreat.

The New Testament, especially Paul in Galatians, says we need to stay in step with the Spirit to be filled with the Spirit. God's presence within us is always looking for an opportunity to bubble up. This spring within us is an eternal source of God's presence within us, God's reality within us, this eternal source that will be there forever. God is looking for a way in which this source can flow from within all that we are to touch all that we encounter.

Some movements have learned how to do that better than others.

And honestly?

It's just like any other discipline. When you encounter folks like this, it's kind of like when you've been eating salty peanuts in a bar. The reason they put out salty peanuts at a bar in England is to make you drink more. The salt makes you thirsty. So you meet these people, and they can look kind of nuts—but they're salty nuts! So you feel like, "Well, they're kind of weird, but I feel like I want to know God better when I'm around them." **It's because the Spirit of God is working through them in such a way that it makes you want to be closer to Jesus.**

I imagine everybody reading this has had at least one eruptive experience of God's presence. It may have been this morning when you saw the sunrise and thought, "Wow, look at that! You're amazing, God! You do this every day! This is incredible." You find your heart exulting and your spirit connecting with the Spirit of God, and you think, "I don't know what it is that I'm saying, God, but I just love you. I'm just overwhelmed." You find yourself overcome, in awe of the majesty, presence, and glory of God.

That may happen in worship, it may happen in nature, it may happen in relationship with others, but everybody has this experience of the eruption of God's presence. If you haven't experienced that, we'll lead you to the Lord later, OK? (I hope you'll allow me this one small joke.)

EROSION

But here's the thing.

This certainly isn't the only place we encounter God's reality and God's presence. And it's certainly not the most frequent.

As I write this, our team just completed our morning Bible text reading in 1 Peter. Peter was concluding his encouragement to the churches he's writing to, mostly in Asia Minor. He was talking in this letter to people who were suffering persecution, and he said, "Just go through this time, because it's going to produce good things."

James, in a similar vein, said, "Count it all joy when you suffer trials of many kinds."[74]

Both were basically saying, "Look, what's happening is that something deeper is taking place in your life. Something more important and significant is going on. The erosive forces of life, the world, the enemy's strategies, are stripping away your life. As this happens it is slowly revealing God's presence."

This is the stripping-away experience of your life, the erosive processes of life.[75] These are just like the erosive forces we see in nature. As your life is stripped away, what's exposed is the presence of God. In Dickens' immortal words, "it was the best of times and the worst of times." How often have we experienced how something is the worst of times, and yet it's the best of times? It's the worst of times in all the circumstances of your life, and yet you feel closer to God now than you have in a long time. What is that? It's the erosion stripping away the surface of your life and exposing the reality of God's presence.

....

[74] James 1:2

[75] In our discipling language, this is D2.

In our moments of greatest weakness, when all has been stripped away, we encounter the perfect power of God's presence. Paul's writings and his story couldn't make that any clearer.

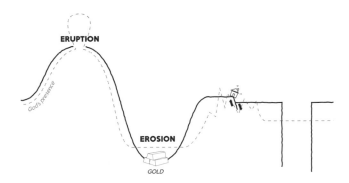

Here is what I have noticed in these times of erosion: our natural inclination toward self-preservation makes us want to get out of the pit as soon as possible. Of course, that's a natural, instinctive, human reaction. But I'd suggest we can take a different posture. You see, as more and more of us is stripped away, what is lying at the bottom of the pit are gold bars that will shape the rest of our lives. They are often the most important things that God is looking to teach us.

So instead of a posture that says, "God, get me out of here as quickly as possible," we step fully into the process and say, "God, don't let me leave this place until I've learned what it is you have to teach."

I was lying in a hospital bed, burns covering my legs, a few years of ministry under my belt with virtually no return, during a time when I was also experiencing erosion in almost every place of my life. In that place, I found a piece of gold that would be an anchor *for the rest of my life*: "LET ME DO IT."

Such a simple word from God. But that time of erosion changed everything as I cried out to God.

Don't leave the times of erosion without the gold. As we talked about with Paul already, the Lord is able to fashion that gold into a crown of righteousness that he places on your head.

EARTHQUAKES

Obviously, the earthquake is a metaphor we've used repeatedly in this book.

As well as the more general experience of "earthquakes" in our culture, we will, from time to time, experience a particular earthquake that hits a fault line in our life. It's not an erosive process that takes place over a long time; it's one of those sudden, shocking things. It could be a death or some kind of catastrophe. It is always a circumstance that jars us to the core.

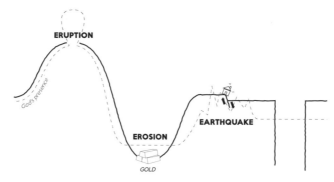

In California, an earthquake hits, and suddenly hot springs bubble up to the surface. Similarly, an earthquake hits your life, and in the midst of it, you suddenly feel the warmth of God's presence. It's almost unexplainable. With David in the Psalms, we see this over and over again. Sometimes I wonder, "How is it that in this time of massive crisis in David's life he was able to experience so much of the presence of God?"

Earlier I mentioned the culture-wide earthquakes that rocked the heart of America with brutalizing force: the Twin Towers falling in the terrorist attack of 9/11 and the twin towers of Banking and Finance falling seven years later.

Now I am not suggesting that God created those circumstances. But it was no accident that immediately following these two events, we saw waves and waves of people come to faith in Christ. The presence of God was already working in their lives, but the earthquake shook something, and their lives were changed.

A few years ago, I was taking a left-hand turn in my tinker-toy of a car at Litchfield Beach and somebody just went through the light at 40 miles per hour and T-boned me. It was the oddest experience. During the crash and after the crash, and honestly 30 minutes later when I needed to give a talk at a 3DM Learning Community, it was like the presence of God was all around me. It was amazing.

I looked at the car, which was now C-shaped, and I thought, "I'm not sure I should have survived that." But somehow, the Lord had not only preserved me, but his presence was also a very real, almost tangible thing.

In the Bible, God's presence is often accompanied by his glory.[76] The Hebrew word for God's presence and glory is *kavod*, which means weight. In times of trouble, we often become aware of God's presence. I have found this often accompanied by a tangible "weighty" sense of God's presence, perhaps explaining the use of the word by Hebrew writers.

EXCAVATION

What do all these things tell us?

They tell us that the task of the Christian believer is to **dig**.

Disciples are meant to dig. The reason we dig is that all of these other experiences tell us that if we dig, the presence of God is always there, sometimes just below the surface. Spiritual disciplines are what we use for excavation.

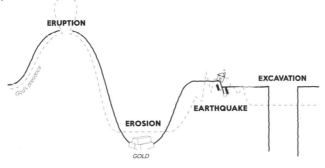

It is not that God is a long way off—he's within us! He's not within everybody. I'm not one of those people who believes that; I just don't think it's a biblical perspective. He can be at work in you, opening you to his work, but you're dead in your sin until you know Jesus. That's reality. But if you know the Lord, and the Lord has claimed you as his own, he lives within you!

....

[76] Exodus 24:15-18

Spiritual disciplines and the journey of the Christian discipleship are means of excavating God's presence. So when we pray, and when we take on other disciplines, we are exposing the presence of God within us and giving God the opportunity to build a conduit through us to touch the lives of the people around us with His presence.[77]

It's as if the spring is uncovered in a well, and the well has a system by which what's in it can be given to others.

Think about teaching or preaching for a moment. What I always teach my leaders, and what I always teach my teams, is this: Preparation is vital. It's part of the excavation. But if you're not speaking out of the overflow of what God is already doing in your life, you're not giving anybody anything. You have to speak out of the overflow of God's presence and God's work in your life.

Think about Paul in Ephesus. He was working 12 hours a day making tents. Do you think he had hours and hours to prepare for his daily teaching at the Hall of Tyrannus? No. It had to come from somewhere deep within, from a place where God was already at work.

This means that if you don't have the opportunity to prepare, you still have something to say. It may not come out very well crafted, but it's still water from the well. John Wesley would always say, "Every Christian should be prepared to preach, pray, or die at a minute's notice." How is that possible? Because you've dug a well, and the water is always available!

So it's not a matter of whether you've had enough time to prepare today, but whether yesterday you did the work of excavation, and the day before that you did the work of excavation, and the day before that you did the work of excavation. If you have been doing that long enough, you have water in the well.

That's what we *have* to go after in our personal lives, and as we live it out in our personal lives, we offer ourselves as an example to others to imitate, so that the whole community can become an oasis of God's presence. We aren't doing it to earn our salvation. This isn't salvation by works. This is stepping

....

[77] I'm not going into tremendous depth on spiritual disciplines when others have done it so well. I can't recommend highly enough Dallas Willard's book *The Spirit of the Disciplines* or Richard Foster's timeless gem *The Celebration of Discipline*.

into the opportunity of a lifetime: walking with Jesus each day and expanding his rule on earth.

Movementally, this is what we are doing with excavation: We are creating channels or canals by which the presence of God can move through us into mission. When we experience the presence of God through earthquake, eruption, or erosion, his presence can move through us into mission because we've already done the hard work of excavation.

I concluded *Multiplying Missional Leaders* with a passage from Ezekiel that showed how there was an eruption of God's presence in the Temple.[78] In this prophetic revelation, the presence of God was represented by a rushing swell of water flowing out of the Temple, out of the city, and in a very particular direction—to the lands of the Gentiles, who were not yet the people of God.

God's heart is always toward those not experiencing his covenantal relationship.

Likewise, in Acts 1 and 2, we see the disciples of Jesus committing themselves to gathering for prayer every day after the Ascension. A corporate discipline. Soon the Holy Spirit came and filled the channels they had dug, and God was able to reach the world through them.

Discipline will lead us to God's presence, and God's presence will lead us into mission—but only if we do the work of excavation in our lives.

Our task is to operate each day in a place of grace that allows us, as we excavate, to slowly create channels and canals of grace that allow us to move out into mission and to take those we are investing in with us.

That's how Paul did it. Not as someone who simply survived or as one trying to earn something. But one who counted it all as joy.

How?

He learned to dig.

....

[78] Ezekiel 47

PART 4

∾ THE MECHANICS ∾ OF A MOVEMENT

Where we've been:
We've laid out the inner journey, through the life of Paul, which must take place in the life of any Kingdom movement leader. We've also used my story as a way of contextualizing what God was doing in and through Paul as a movement was being birthed in Ephesus. We see that it is a commitment for the long haul, "a long obedience in the same direction."

Where we are going:
In Part 4, we will begin to explore some of the nuts-and-bolts of how to build a sustainable Kingdom movement.

12

～ ORBITAL PATTERNS, HIGGS ～ BOSON, AND MOLASSES

I wonder, sometimes, if the Lord gives us something early on that really grabs our attention so that it can serve as a foundation for the rest of our life. It's as if we live the rest of our lives through that specific lens of revelation.

For Sally and me, that has certainly been the case.

Much of what I have shared from the life of Paul are things that we've learned over the last 35 to 40 years as we've studied the scriptures, gathering insights by slowly living out what we saw there.

But very early in our marriage, something that Paul did stood out. Since then, it has served as a mooring—a grounding point for Sally and me in all that we've done.

It won't sound revolutionary initially, but here it is: **Paul's missionary life was laid out in orbital patterns.**

If you read Acts 11 through 21, you will notice, over and over again, certain patterns guiding Paul's life.

For instance, as someone who was part of something larger than himself, after every missionary journey, he orbited into his missional sending center. He always returned to Antioch or

MISSIONAL SENDING CENTERS:
Communities that have enough spiritual mass, with leaders who embody the character and competency of Jesus, that they become places of training, sending and reproduction for leaders into the missional frontier, as well as a safe harbor of orbit for those coming from the missional frontier.

Jerusalem. Each time, he'd spend at least a year there before going out again.

By the time Paul established the church in Ephesus, these orbital patterns were well established.

He set up similar orbital patterns for members of his team and seemed to do this in three distinct ways.

First, as we've already seen, his team orbited into times with him each and every day before being sent out each day. Second, he (and no doubt his team) regularly visited the growing number of distant households multiplying across the city. Third, he had his team do the same thing in microcosm that he did after each missionary journey. He sent his teams off to plant churches, carry letters, and represent him—only to orbit back into the missional sending center he was building in Ephesus.

Let's make sure we understand what is happening here, because this is all about reproduction, a key element of any movement. Paul reproduced himself in his leaders, and they continued to orbit into his life regularly. These orbital patterns were then extrapolated into the whole missionary enterprise.

Sometimes we assume that reproduction means disconnection where you're constantly saying goodbye. But in a healthy reproducing movement, you're never really saying goodbye; instead, you're saying *see you later*. You will be seeing these people again. No matter how big the enterprise, you should always orbit into something that is bigger than *your thing*.

In my experience, the more Character and Competency that have been formed in the leader we have multiplied, the longer the orbital pattern. He or she doesn't need to orbit in as much. However, if we are seeing our *oikos* just starting to shape, train, and deploy a new leader, I'm going to want him or her to orbit in much more often.

Like I said, this may not sound revolutionary, but it has proved revolutionary in Sally's and my life and ministry together in the last 35 to 40 years. Practically speaking, here is how it plays out:

We have always and continue to have team prayers together every single working day. Every day the whole team (often times with kids too) gathers together for 30 minutes. We worship together, listen to the Lord together, open the Scriptures together, and pray for the day together. That's how we start our day of work.

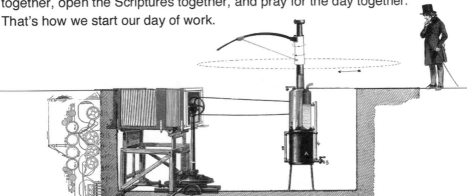

We would have regular Huddles with the 8-10 leaders in whom we were most directly investing at the time, while also inviting them into our home and life outside of this discipleship-focused Huddle time. As each of those leaders had Huddles of leaders as well, we asked them to have their leaders orbiting into their lives regularly too.

At St. Thomas, we asked our Missional Community leaders to orbit into our worship service at least once a month but no more than three times a month (to ensure they were at least out on mission one Sunday a month).

In recent years, the leaders we trained have used Learning Communities to establish this orbital pattern. In these Learning Communities, we gather the leaders of those Missional Communities together every six months for a Friday and Saturday, creating a type of retreat where they can evaluate what the Lord was saying to their community and what the next six months need to be about. We would invest heavily in these retreats and pour our very best into these leaders.

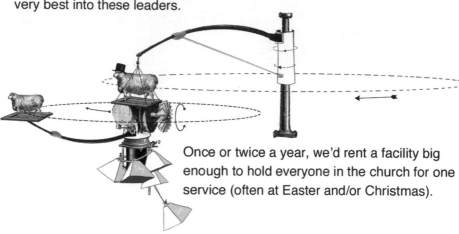

Once or twice a year, we'd rent a facility big enough to hold everyone in the church for one service (often at Easter and/or Christmas).

We are part of a larger community called The Order of Mission (TOM), a covenant community of Kingdom leaders that is a neo-monastic movement. Every three years we gather the whole family of missionary leaders (more than 600) from all six continents together in one place. And even more often than that, members of TOM have regular regional gatherings each year.

Orbiting patterns shape our lives. I truly believe that predictable rhythms of orbiting patterns are the only thing that can give us the "freedom in the framework" we need to birth a Kingdom movement.

So in Sally's and my life right now, there are orbiting patterns of:

Daily

Weekly

Monthly

Semi-Annually

Annually

Tri-Annually

The whole movement is beginning to see similar patterns emerge, all across the world. Once you recognize the value of those orbits and patterns, it is fairly easy to replicate and multiply them.

Now again, this isn't revolutionary.

Many people have seen things like this before or are in particular denominations where the whole system of doing church is predicated on this thought. But I want to make sure we emphasize this idea, because it is crucial to every movement. We need to be intentional about it! But the key is that these things are flexible. What we don't want happening is that things crystallize in such a way that we become immovable, or falsely believe there is a model or system that automatically produces a movement.

Europe was evangelized because in the Synod of Whitby in AD 664, the Roman and the Celtic church expressions created concentric orbital patterns. In time, this created the "Minsters" of England: monastic missional centers of spiritual life and vitality that defined European Christendom for hundreds of years.

As this movement grew, it materialized into some of the patterns we saw in the medieval church. They had communion every day in their local village church with maybe 30-40 people. They met together for worship on Sunday. A few times a year, the village church would caravan together for a festival to the Cathedral—perhaps at Christmas, Easter, or to celebrate a patron saint.

And then maybe once or twice in their lifetime, they took a pilgrimage to a special pilgrimage site like Canterbury or Chartres.

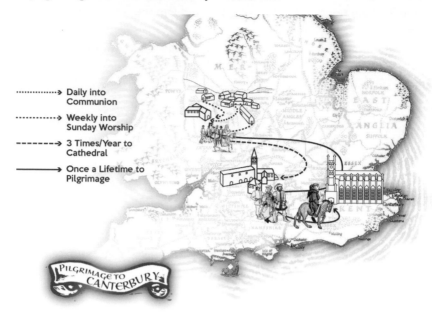

We find similar patterns in Jewish religious life. Disciples met with their rabbi daily. On the Sabbath, the village gathered in the synagogue. Several times a year the village traveled to the Temple in Jerusalem for Passover, the Festival of First Fruits, etc.

John Wesley created a "method" that re-evangelized large areas of England and the United States with similar orbital patterns.

Missionary agencies in the 20th century sent their missionaries out for several years and then had them orbit into the central sending center for a period of time on "furlough".

Our missional history is built on these orbital patterns, and it's all coming out of what we see in the life of Paul.

But let me throw out one thing that I believe does make this truly revolutionary: at the beating heart of all of these orbital patterns should be a missional *oikos*—itself formed by orbital patterns. When we build the orbital patterns of movement in this way (and with *oikos* at its heart), we get closer to the genius and success of the early church.

In the Middle Ages, this principle was established through the Missionary Orders—the army of sacrificial celibate men and women who evangelized the known world. At the heart of this movement was the "family" of brothers and sisters overseen by an "Abba", who, following the founders of the movement, functioned as the spiritual parent of the family.[79] **At no point in this orbital pattern are we to be removed from our participation in an *oikos*—ever.**

Oikos—an extended family on mission—is the beating heart of the movement!

When I was the Rector of St. Thomas, I met a precocious and enormously gifted woman named Joannah. She was a 20-year-old university student when I met her. She came from a pretty difficult and broken background, and Sally and I felt called to invest in her. The next thing we knew, Jo was showing up to our house almost every day—*coincidentally* right around the time we were having dinner. Fair enough. We could give the kid some food. After all, mealtimes are the center of family life—and this was a great way for us to connect.

As it turns out, Jo is one of the most incredible leaders I've ever met.

She started out discipling some other girls (including our daughters!). Then she led a Missional Community. Then she started a college ministry that exploded, followed by many more adventures in mission.

Today, Jo Saxton is one of the most sought-after speakers and leaders in the United Kingdom and the United States. She has just landed in Minnesota, where she and her husband are joining forces with North Heights Church to help build a Kingdom movement among young adults. Mark my words—it will be *amazing*.

When we first met her, Jo orbited into our life every day. As time passed and the character and competency of Jesus increased in her, she began to orbit in a little less. She moved to once a week. She and her family ended up moving to the United States with us when we left the UK, and they spent time on a team with us. Then they went on to spend some time in California before moving to Minnesota.

....

[79] Male was Abbot; female was Abbess. Both mean "Papa," though not to speak to gender. Rather, to speak of how they might be seen as a picture of our great Papa, God the Father.

Now Sally and I live in Pawleys Island, South Carolina, and Jo is thousands of miles away in the land of 10,000 lakes. But we are still connected, still part of the same Kingdom movement within 3DM and The Order of Mission. And beyond that, we still feel like Jo, her husband Chris, and their kids are *part of our family*. They just are.

She has an *oikos* of her own and is starting movements of her own, much like Paul's guys did in Acts 19. So her orbital pattern has changed. But I still get texts from her a few times a week, and we talk on the phone regularly. And at least every three to six months, she orbits into our life in Pawleys or on the road somewhere.

Now I am not suggesting that everyone you are currently investing in will be in your *oikos* for the rest of your life. Quite the contrary, many of the people the Lord has given to you will be with you for a season before they are released. But I think we all have people we know, no matter where they live, who will be in our *oikos* for the rest of our lives.

Will the orbital patterns change? Of course. Will these people go on to start things of their own, reproducing what you have taught them and starting their own *oikos*? Of course! That's the point. In fact, we should expect them to do even greater things. That's what we're aiming for.

But you will be family with them for the rest of your life. And if you are able to build your life on these orbital patterns, always connecting you and your *oikos*, you will find it has the capacity be ever expanding, joining a movement that is changing the world—one that is bringing heaven to earth.

HIGGS BOSON AND MOLASSES

For years, I've lived out this orbital pattern and seen the movemental effects it has in all sizes of Kingdom community. But it wasn't until a few months ago that I felt the Lord gave me a picture of what is really happening with people in these patterns. *I knew they were important, but I couldn't quite put my finger on what exactly was happening when people and groups orbited through our lives.* You know how it is. You see something, and you know it resonates with scripture, your instincts, and your experience. But that doesn't necessarily mean you understand what's happening at a foundational level.

That's how it was with orbital patterns. I knew *oikos* was at the center of it and it provided a framework for sustainable reproduction, but I knew there was more to it as well.

Then, a few months ago, I saw something in the news that captured my interest: they finally found the Higgs boson.

For quite some time, scientists have debated the origins of the universe and why the universe continues to have expanding mass.

First, there was nothing.

No mass at all in the whole universe. But at some point, the mass had to come from somewhere, right? If there was nothing, and then there was something, and that mass continues to slowly expand over time, what created this phenomenon? Of course, we know that God created it. But the logical question any physicist would ask is, "how?"

The hypothesis of many particle physicists was that a field was created at the advent of the universe that involved a Higgs boson particle (often referred to as the *God particle*). When other particles, which contain no mass, passed through this field, they gained mass—sort of like how a pea might gain mass as it travels through molasses.

When the pea enters the molasses field, the pea has a certain mass. But when the pea leaves, it has some of the molasses with it, increasing the pea's overall mass.

In the 1980s, scientists built the underground, 10-kilometer circular Hadron Collider near the France–Switzerland border. Then in 1998, they built another one that was 27 kilometers long called the Large Hadron Collider (costing something in the area of $6.2 billion). For 30 years, they have been smashing accelerated atomic particles into each other, trying to recreate this phenomenon, searching for the God particle. It has formed what is probably one of the most expensive and universally sought-after experiments for physics since the Manhattan Project.

In the spring of 2012, the scientists at CERN[80] popped the corks and sprayed champagne everywhere because finally, after 30 years searching, they had found the Higgs boson particle. They re-created the invisible field that gives mass-less particles mass. It is truly one of the most astonishing finds in all of scientific history. *Higgsteria* became a worldwide phenomenon.[81] (To illustrate the degree to which this captivated the world, here are a few pictorial examples.)

For whatever reason, this continued to settle in my heart and imagination. One day, the Lord put these two things together—orbital patterns of *oikos* and the Higgs boson, and it all became clear. An invisible field that gives mass when objects travel through it explains *perfectly* why the orbital pattern is central to any Kingdom movement.

Whether you are orbiting into someone's *oikos*, a Missional Community orbiting into a worship service, a leader orbiting into a Learning Community every six months, or the whole church gathering together once a year in one place in one worship service, each is an instance in which, by orbiting through something with the right properties, *we gain mass because we've orbited into something that gives increased mass in our ability to go out into mission*. Like the pea entering the molasses, we take some of the mass with us.

As we enter the field of God's presence and power in the life of a particular community (however large), we are formed by it and empowered for greater impact in the world. We all know intuitively that much of what is important in life is "more caught than taught." But this metaphor seems to provide an

[80] This project is headed by CERN, the European Organization for Nuclear Research. It was started in 1954 in the suburbs of Geneva, Switzerland, and is backed by 20 European countries.

[81] This was CNN's terrible pun, not my own!

insight into how this happens. I had long known that missional activity apart from these orbital patterns was futile. It's not sustainable. This new analogy was a window into why this was the case.

Viscerally, I think we all actually "get" this analogy.

Most of us have experienced a time when we orbited into something bigger than ourselves and had a sense that we left with more mass than what we came in with. For example, say you spent an evening having dinner with a married couple who are older than you and who have followed Jesus for a *long* time. When you think about what Jesus might have looked like, you imagine he probably looked a lot like them. Then you notice that when you leave, you have a strange sensation that *something of them* was coming with you.

It's like the pea going through the molasses. Orbiting through the molasses allowed you to carry some of the molasses with you upon leaving, essentially *giving you more of the mass of Jesus.*

As we mentioned earlier, the Hebrew word for glory is *kavod*, which means "weight." So when Moses was exposed to the glory of the Lord in the cleft of the rock, he not only shone with the glory of God but also carried the weight of the presence of the Lord with him.[82]

Another word we sometimes use (though not always well) to describe this phenomenon is *gravitas*. People and communities carry this kind of weight, and we say they have a certain *gravitas* to them.

Something else is also going on here. We aren't simply gaining spiritual mass through these orbital patterns for the sake of gaining mass. **We are learning how to create mass so we can do the same.**

As people and communities enter into a missional sending center, we become people capable of launching more centers. And more centers. And more centers. It's reproduction on every level.

If we want to start Kingdom movements, we don't just need orbital patterns; we need orbital patterns into centers of mission that have real spiritual mass.

....

[82] Exodus 33:21-13, Exodus 34:29-31

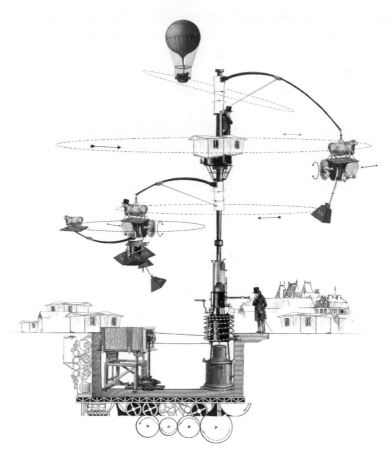

They need to have a "weightiness" to them. *A gravitas* in the community.

And at the center of it will be an *oikos*, creating that kind of culture and community. This community has weight, mass, *gravitas*.

I'm not talking about celebrity.

Hear me very clearly: this isn't about finding a celebrity.

In fact, the people in my life I've come into contact with who have the most spiritual mass *aren't people you'd know*. Why? Because it's never about them. The spiritual realm operates just like Higgs boson where there is a field. The invitation is gravitation toward the center of that person's life. The challenge is that as you collect spiritual mass to yourself, you are naturally pushed out in a manner that will propel you away (through the natural orbital pattern).

That person or that community isn't the point. The gravitational field of spiritual mass isn't the point. The point is that Jesus is at the center, welcomed and honored, and he becomes the gravitational force that draws and the centrifugal force that sends out. Jesus is always about invitation to community and challenge to change the world!

Of course the spiritual disciples alluded to in the previous section are vital to all of this. Orbital patterns are made from rhythms and disciplines of life that welcome Jesus as the gravitational center of our lives together.

And here lies the problem for many of us: we can create orbital patterns. We might even be able to create an *oikos*. But that doesn't mean we have the spiritual mass in our community yet that would allow people to gain mass by orbiting through it and sending them out.

Most of us don't have the faintest clue how to create spiritual mass.

1 3

∾ RED-HOT CENTERS ∾

∙∙∙

We have just seen how spiritual mass is essential to creating the kinds of *oikos* and communities that will birth Kingdom movements. ***But how do we do this?***

Michael Green's excellent book *Thirty Years that Changed the World* has helped me understand this at a more concrete level. Allow me to share an excerpt:

> *The approach of the first Christians was strikingly different* [than our modern way of evangelizing]. *It was a totally opposite strategy* [than how we do "outreach"]. *They learned it from Jesus. He had spent much quality time with three men; Peter, James and John. Beyond that had been the circle of the twelve, then of the seventy, then of the crowds. Jesus had concentrated on getting the center of his little band hot and well informed, and he moved out from there. And that is what the disciples did. They gave attention to their own unity and prayerfulness, obedience, and expectancy. And they were able to move out from that **hot center** onto the streets with enormous effect on the day of Pentecost and in the months and years that followed. In obedience to Jesus, they began to be his witness in Jerusalem first, then Judea, then Samaria and then to the uttermost ends of the earth. It was an effective strategy. **Their fellowship was so vibrant, their lifestyle so attractive, their warmth so great that it was infectious.** People were drawn in, as to a vortex. God added to the church those who were being saved.*

I'd like to develop the metaphor a little to help us understand spiritual mass.

After all, if we need to create spiritual mass on an individual, family, extended family, and missional sending center level, we had best understand it.

When you increase gravity and mass, you usually create heat. So when we think of the places we are orbiting, let's think of them as red-hot centers.

Acts 5:12-16 will help us do this:

> The apostles performed many signs and wonders among the people. And all the believers used to meet together in Solomon's Colonnade. No one else dared join them, even though they were highly regarded by the people. Nevertheless, more and more men and women believed in the Lord and were added to their number. As a result, people brought the sick into the streets and laid them on beds and mats so that at least Peter's shadow might fall on some of them as he passed by. Crowds gathered also from the towns around Jerusalem, bringing their sick and those tormented by impure spirits, and all of them were healed.

Did you catch that?

The people were *scared to death* of what was happening, and *no else dared join them*. But they couldn't help themselves. They couldn't stay away. The gravitational pull of this red-hot center was so strong that, even though everyone did his or her best not to be around these people, they couldn't. They kept coming. That's how strong the gravitational field was. More people became disciples. More people were healed. More people were delivered.

How fascinating is that?! Isn't that what we long for in our communities?

In the book of Acts, three red-hot centers clearly emerge: Jerusalem, Antioch, and Ephesus. Each served as a missional sending center for missionaries, church planters, and movement creators. The reason those sent could do these incredible things was because of what they had learned in the red-hot center.

It will come as no great shock to you if you have read any of my previous books or blogs that, as I've studied this phenomenon, I think there are three things at work in creating a red-hot sending center—and of course they fit on a triangle.

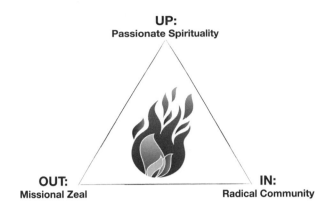

UP:
Passionate Spirituality

OUT:
Missional Zeal

IN:
Radical Community

Passionate Spirituality: In each place, the church was absolutely passionate about God. That passion was expressed in unbridled praise and worship, prayer, commitment to the teaching and obeying of the word, and lives oriented around fasting, feasting, and the breaking of bread.

Radical Community: In each place, vibrant expressions of community existed. People were prepared to sacrifice and share life to levels that we would call extreme today, in order to be a family on mission together.

Missional Zeal: We see a movement of mission develop in each place, with each having a slightly different flavor. In Jerusalem, the church saw people added to their number daily, and it seems like it happened more because of their life of radical community. Antioch enjoyed the presence of many missionaries and very large evangelistic gatherings. Ephesus sent out church planters and movement leaders in their own right.

These three elements were present in each church. When we practice these things, they reflect the life of Jesus, and by practicing these expressions of his life consistently, we reveal we are his disciples and welcome his presence among us.

As we've discussed already, each thing happened on the continuum of Organized and Organic, of a Temple expression and the home. Passionate spirituality in a home with 30 people is certainly different from in the Temple of Jerusalem with 3,000. By the same token, radical community with a group of 3,000 looks different from radical community with a group of 30.

These three churches were committed to this kind of life on every level. And as they did this, as the Holy Spirit breathed his life onto the burning embers of this community, a raging bonfire started to roar.

We can imagine a fireplace bellow being squeezed as the Holy Spirit breathed life onto the community as it scatters, and then retracting as the community gathered back together for worship and praise, making the fire hotter and hotter. This scattered reality of mission and the gathered reality of locating yourself within a much larger story are essential to the red-hot center.

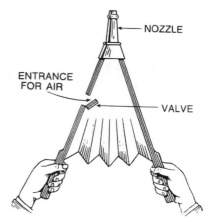

The early church was structured so that people were given access to a household on mission that was still small enough to get close to the fire. Often our churches are structured so that only the privileged few really get in on the action.

This is the beauty of Missional Communities.

TORCHES

Imagine that a red-hot center is burning at the center of every MC as a sort of torch. (Or perhaps in your context, every torch represents a church planter, campus pastor, movement leader, or missionary.)

The thing with torches is that they are really portable.

For Missional Communities,

that's really important. A Missional Community, by definition, finds a crack or crevice in society that is dark and incarnates a Jesus community there, slipping into that crevice with the torch of the gospel. You can't fit a giant bonfire in that crack; only a torch will work. So the flexibility and portability of the torch are incredibly important.

However, torches also go out fairly easy. One little rainstorm will put it out. Although torches are portable, without proper care, they will burn out within a short amount of time. And even if the torch doesn't burn out, it will sputter and become far less bright than it once was. People don't tend to gravitate toward torches that are burning out. They lose the invitation of the burning fire.

This is why there is a dire missional need for these torches to regularly gather together so that they aren't simply torches scattered along the missional frontier, slowly flickering out. By coming together, we can actually become a raging bonfire that continues to burn hotter and brighter when we return to the missional frontier. There are times when the torch needs to go out and **do**, as well as times when the torches need to come together, create a giant fire, feeding from the flames of the gathered company, and just **be**.

We see this continuum in the Jerusalem church. The followers of Jesus' primary expression of church were in the home as they broke bread, did life together, and cared for each other. These households were the primary focus of mission throughout the New Testament era. However, in Jerusalem (and probably in Ephesus, per Acts 19:1) these extended family churches also all came together to gather at the Temple regularly. So you had Temple and home, and both needed the other to find their proper place.

We gather and then we scatter. We gather and we scatter. The bellows of the Holy Spirit continue to work.

BUILDING A RED-HOT CENTER

How do you build a red-hot center?

It is simple, but hard to do. (As opposed to complex, but easy to do.)

Building a red-hot center requires that you change the way you understand what your community is supposed to be doing in this world. That will require significant work in you as a leader, in terms of what the Lord wants to do in you and what he is able to do *through you* as a leader.

First, let's examine the community aspect.

Leaders must attend to having a "gathered expression" of church that has all three elements: Passionate Spirituality (UP), Radical Community (IN), and Missional Zeal (OUT). Scattered expressions of church—in the extended family size—should have all three as well.

This picture of gathering and scattering (of the inhaling of the Spirit bringing us together and his exhaling sending us out) takes those small burning embers and, in time, ignites them into a red-hot center—a burning inferno of God's presence and power.

Again, this is much easier said than done.

As we look at the church landscape around us, we generally see churches are usually committed to two of the three things, while often paying lip service to the third (or not even acknowledging it at all).

Interestingly, this is what we see in the book of Acts as well.

Jerusalem was a church that did UP and IN very well. People gathered every day in the Temple courts and from house to house for prayer, teaching, the Lord's Supper, and worship. The people shared everything they had with each other, and everyone's needs were cared for.

But mission didn't seem to come naturally, and in the end, getting the church to reach out toward the Gentiles and "the ends of the earth" took serious pressure. Persecution happened. People were scattered and scared to death.

Antioch was a church that did UP and OUT very well. By all accounts, it was a very large church, probably numbering in the thousands. Archaeologists who discovered the place where the church met seem to agree with this assertion. The church was committed to teaching, fasting, and prayer, and truly embraced the spiritual disciplines, taking UP very seriously.

In addition, Antioch was certainly a sending center for missionaries. This seemed to always be on the mind of the leaders at Antioch. This probably had a lot to do with Barnabas, whom Luke mentioned in Acts 11 and Acts 13, as someone either looking for a partner in missionary work or being sent out by the church. We know from future chapters that Antioch continued to be a sending center for missionaries and a place for them to rest between journeys.

But with all the talk of UP and OUT, we find next to no mention of the IN-ward dimension of the life of the church in Antioch.

Now I don't want to suggest that there was no IN-ward dimension in Antioch or no OUT-ward in Jerusalem. My sense is that the Holy Spirit is highlighting aspects of their lives that we should look for in *every church*. But it is nevertheless quite curious that each church had two of the three dimensions mentioned so effusively, while conspicuously omitting a third dimension. I find that interesting.

But in Ephesus, as we've already examined with our overview of the missional work of Paul, we see UP, IN, and OUT at work.

Of the three model churches in Acts, in many ways Ephesus develops a red-hot center with fewer resources than either Jerusalem or Antioch and, thus, is perhaps the church most worthy of study.

Why am I so committed to all three things being present? (Besides the fact that any expression of church should be patterned after these three dimensions of Jesus' life?)

This is why: if you're committed to passionate spirituality and radical community but not missional zeal, you will get a community that becomes insular, that increasingly looks inward, that slowly becomes obsessed with self-preservation and legacy, and that over time will die out. Literally. The people in the community pass away, and the community dies with them. Whole denominations attest to this.

If you're committed to passionate spirituality and missional zeal but not radical community, you miss the primary vehicle that God uses to bring his Kingdom to earth and expresses himself in human form: the *Christian extended family*. You will get a community of individualistic missional ninjas who better resemble an atomized, ill-formed monastic order. Only the radicals may enter. **Turnover will be high because of the high emphasis on mission. Without a playful, vibrant community, sustaining your calling will be difficult.**

If you're committed to radical community and missional zeal but not passionate spirituality, you're not missing anything too important—just an intimate, life-giving relationship with our Father who honored the presence of Jesus and then released the power of the Holy Spirit! The Holy Spirit is the only means by which our cry "Your will be done on earth as it is in heaven" can ever come to fruition. After all, it was Jesus who said, "Apart from me, you can do nothing." And "I will send you the Holy Spirit"—the *Paraclete*.

Often we either get numbers focused or become quasi-obsessed with social justice. Both are important. More people in Heaven and fewer people in Hell is important. Changing the way the world works and standing on the side of the weak and the poor, seeing the chains of injustice loosed, is vital. *But how are we supposed to do that apart from the Holy Spirit?*

Neither is sustainable. Churches obsessed with converts and creating community won't see transformation, either communally or individually, because they are missing the change agent of the Holy Spirit. Eventually, people realize they bought into something that you can't deliver.

Churches focused with communal change and social justice without passionate spirituality lack the same change agent: the invited presence and power of the Holy Spirit. Let's be very clear: we will not be able to loose the chains of injustice without the power of the Holy Spirit. We don't have it in us.

It must be all three, at the gathered level and the scattered level.

RETURNING TO THE MOUNT

Let's say for instance that we find ourselves in a community that might not be as committed to these three as they could be. Just hypothetically, of course. And let's say that as a result, our community resembles a small marshmallow roast rather than a raging bonfire that can be described as a red-hot center for God's presence and power.

What do we do about it?

The first thing to realize is that we are dealing with a spiritual problem. What we are trying to do is gain more spiritual mass.

This is a human problem common to us all, but we need to understand it in a different way. We need to realize that the Holy Spirit wants our communities to have spiritual mass far more than we do and that he is already at work. *He is already at work!* The key is finding where he is at work in that place and joining him in it. It is always more about the grace of God taking the initiative to lead than our human effort!

What we need to do is **find the grace**.

The typical answer you might find in a book on Christian leadership is the newest fad, strategic vehicle, or silver-bullet solution. I don't have that for you. But what I can offer is the same thing that Jesus offered his disciples—his teaching.

When Jesus taught, he offered particular insights at particular times that helped the disciples understand what they needed to understand about particular situations. Every so often, he gave general teaching, and in this, he revealed the complete picture of what he was actually calling them to.

One such teaching was what we call "The Lord's Prayer." Of course, the Lord's Prayer is set within a "bigger" message often called "The Sermon on the Mount," in which Jesus outlined the expectations he has for his followers. In the Lord's Prayer, Jesus not only brings his teaching on prayer together but also provides a lens through which we can understand all that he wanted to say.

Matthew 6:9-13

> *This, then, is how you should pray:*
> *Our Father in heaven,*
> *hallowed be your name,*

your kingdom come,
your will be done,
on earth as it is in heaven.
Give us today our daily bread.
And forgive us our debts,
as we also have forgiven our debtors.
And lead us not into temptation,
but deliver us from the evil one.

What we see in this model are six points of focus that we can pray through over and over again[83]:

The Father's Character: Help us know you in such a way that we always know and experience the innate goodness of your character. "If you, though you are evil, give good gifts to your kids, how much more so will your father in heaven give you the best things?"[84]

The Father is the King of a Kingdom: Help us to advance your Kingdom through your Holy Spirit in such a way that we fight "not against flesh and blood, but against the powers and principalities." We are in a spiritual battle. Things exist in Heaven in a certain way—may they exist that way on earth![85]

The Father's Provision: Help us with the things we need each day! We need food, shelter, jobs. We need community and family. Provide us the things we need spiritually, emotionally, and physically. "You prepare a table before me in the presence of my enemies. You anoint my head with oil; my cup overflows."[86]

The King's Forgiveness: Help us to forgive others the way you have forgiven us, and in doing so allow us to accept and experience your forgiveness. May I exist in a community where forgiveness abounds and grace reigns. "For if you can't love your brother who you can see, how can you love God whom you cannot see?"[87]

....

[83] For more on these focus points, see the chapter on the Lord's Prayer in the book *Building a Discipling Culture*.

[84] Matthew 7:11

[85] Ephesians 6:12

[86] Psalm 23:5

[87] 1 John 4:20

The Father's Protection: Help us to remain pure and set apart as we step out into a broken world each day. "For you were once darkness, but now you are light in the Lord. Live as children of light."[88] May our hearts beat with your heart, longing for all of the good things for which you long.

The King's Deliverance: Help us to fight well against the principalities and powers, with your Holy Spirit leading us. And when we get into the thick of it, deliver us as no one else can but you. For we know that "our enemy prowls around like a roaring lion, looking for someone to devour."[89]

When we understand how Jesus was asking us to pray, we start to see that these things start to group together in a certain way. The six emphases of the Lord's Prayer can be grouped into two groups of three phrases. Each group focuses on the Covenant of the Father and the Kingdom of the King. We start to see that praying like this has implications for us, our family, our extended spiritual family, and the wider spiritual community of which we are part.

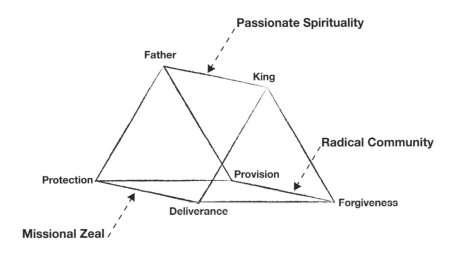

If we arrange these Covenant and Kingdom phrases like this, we can see a connection with passionate spirituality, radical community, and missional zeal.

It's all connected.

....

88 Ephesians 5:8
89 1 Peter 5:8

Now that we have seen the importance of prayer, let's begin to address specific issues that come when our communities lack passionate spirituality, radical community, and missional zeal. **As we do, remember that we are dealing with spiritual realities, and thus, we must approach any solution with that understanding.**

GROWING IN PASSIONATE SPIRITUALITY

If we are lacking in **passionate spirituality**, we see in the Lord's Prayer how we can build that place of weakness: by focusing on the Father's Character and the King's Kingdom. So we pray that our hearts would be oriented more and more toward the heart of God. We pray that we would understand him as a good dad who wants the very best for us, and that we can trust him. And as we trust him, we go out into the world and represent him as the Holy Spirit works in us.

I think a lot of it is that we just can't wrap our heads around what our Father is doing for us. He has given us an identity that says he's already proud of us. He believes in us. *When he sees us, what he sees is Jesus.* We are caught up in that!

One of the most helpful ways of engaging with this is to remember that because of the covenant relationship we have with Jesus, everything the Father says to Jesus, he says to us. Read the baptism of Jesus in Matthew 4. Read the Transfiguration in Mark 9. Read how God attended to Jesus in Luke 22 as he's preparing for the cross. *Everything that the Father says to Jesus, he says to you.*

It causes our hearts to swell with a sense of the Father's delight in us. He wants to glorify himself because of you. You see, Security leads to Significance. If you want to understand why people are able to do significant things, it's because they are secure in their relationship with the Father.

From that, we realize there is royal blood flowing through our veins. We are kids of the King. And like any royal family member, we now represent the King; we represent because we are family, which means we are enormously committed to what we're doing. We are helping to build the kingdom that is being given to us. In the way that Jesus covenanted a kingdom to his disciples in Luke 22,[90] he is looking to do the same for us.

People who are building something that is theirs tend to have a greater commitment to it than something that isn't. Every statistic in the world shows how people are far more productive when they have ownership of something.

I'm fully convinced that when the new heaven and the new earth are joined together for all of eternity, *we will be able to recognize the work of our hands in this life*. What you're doing is extending the Kingdom, and that is eternal fruit, fruit that won't fade or pass. You will be able to recognize your work!

GROWING IN RADICAL COMMUNITY

If we are lacking in **radical community**, we assume practices that are simply but powerfully spoken of in this prayer: forgive each other, receive forgiveness, and pray for provision (the Father's Provision and the King's Forgiveness).

Now, we can't understand these prayers in a vacuum. The Bible *always* understands provision within the context of community. *Always.* You are not your own.

You belong to a family, and that family looks out for you as you look out for the other members of the family. The prayer implies not only that you should pray for provision, but also that you expect that the answer could come from your extended family.

Another thing at work with provision is an understanding that other members of our extended families are praying for the exact same thing, and we have the opportunity to be an answer to their prayers.

It is not by accident that the early church produced this kind of community: "All the believers were together and had everything in common. They sold

....

[90] Luke 22:29-30. *And I confer on you a kingdom, just as my Father conferred one on me, so that you may eat and drink at my table in my kingdom and sit on thrones, judging the twelve tribes of Israel.*

property and possessions to give to anyone who had need."[91] **They were simply living out what such a prayer would imply! This is the result of praying seriously! It's absolutely amazing.**

Let's not leave out forgiveness, both giving it and accepting it for ourselves. This is clearly a community ethic for Jesus. That's why he highlights it again in practical detail in Matthew 18: "Look, this is how you deal with situations when someone has sinned against you. Go straight to them. Deal with the issue. Always seek forgiveness and reconciliation!"[92]

In Part 2, in my story, I referenced what happened at St. Tom's. In 10 years, not a single divorce. That's the natural end for a community that takes forgiveness and reconciliation seriously and deals with it quickly.

Sometimes I think we tend to have a rather *effete* view of sin. We associate sin with the Father rather than with the King. It's the judgment seat of the King that we are released from. Salvation means that we are not judged. Our lives are held up to see what we've achieved, but our salvation is secure because we are not coming to the judgment seat of the King. We've been exonerated. Absolutely, as we read in things like the Parable of the Talents, we'll be asked, "What have you done?" But salvation is not at risk because the King has declared us forgiven. We are released. Mercy has been given.

What we are doing when we sin is actually violating that relationship with the King. It's the King we are offending. It's not a push-over daddy to whom we are saying we are sorry. We've broken the King's law, but he's generous enough to give us his grace. It's such a sobering thing.

Taking the prayer for Provision and Forgiveness seriously means we take it down into what it means for the communities we lead and of which we are part.

GROWING IN MISSIONAL ZEAL

Now if we are talking about **missional zeal** as a weakness, we see in the Lord's Prayer an implicit statement: you need only Protection and Deliverance

....

[91] Acts 2:43-44
[92] Matthew 18:15

if you're going OUT into the full brokenness of the world. Let's be really clear on this. If you are staying in the relatively safe quarters of the church building, our enemy just isn't that concerned about you. I promise you, he isn't! There really isn't that much Protection or Deliverance needed if you're in the Christian refugee camps.

So let's expound the prayer for what Jesus is implying: "And when we go OUT, keep us protected from the temptations that swirl around us. And when we engage with our enemy and feel overwhelmed, deliver us from his clutches. May we win the battle!"

We have to go OUT. It's just not an option. So as we go out, we continue to return to this prayer over and over again. Protect us, deliver us. Protect us, deliver us.

Here's the question: Where is God calling you to go OUT? Where is his Spirit already at work? Go join him there, and as you go, pray, "Protect us, deliver us. Protect us, deliver us."

There's just not a lot to say here, you know? Listen to the voice of the Great Shepherd. Hear the call of the Warrior King. Find where his Kingdom is already breaking in and join him there. Go!

This prayer we are taught to pray *presupposes* we are patterning our life and the life of our community after Jesus, that we're doing the things he's about. The prayer is simply inviting the Holy Spirit into a life already oriented around Kingdom living. Perhaps for many of us, the issue remains that there are parts of us still not oriented toward King Jesus and his coming Kingdom.

SELF-DIAGNOSIS

One last thought: The interesting reality about these three things is that whatever weakness your community is seeing is usually mirrored in your own life first. The principle of "Leaders define culture" is not an accident. So whether you are seeing weakness in passionate spirituality, radical community, or missional zeal, please know that there is a process in seeing breakthrough for your weakness in your community:

- **Start in your own life.** How is your weakness mirrored in the culture you are creating? In what way is Jesus inviting you to change? Where is he looking to bring breakthrough in your life first?

- **Let the breakthrough spread.** Let it start with your nuclear family and then spread to your extended spiritual family. I've seen it over and over again: the breakthrough that I receive personally spreads to my spouse, kids, and the *oikos* I'm part of.

- **Breakthrough abounds.** Revelation 12 tells us that we win by "the blood of Jesus and the word of our testimony." So when you receive breakthrough, when you see it in your family and in your *oikos*, tell some stories and invite people into this greater reality.

I cannot say it long enough or loud enough: you must lead from your own brokenness so that, as the Lord achieves breakthrough in your life and those you are close to, he will use the overflow of that in the wider community.

When I sensed that the Lord was asking me to carry the cross in the inner city in Brixton Hill, God was confronting something wired deep within me: I *hated* looking foolish in front of other people. Because so many of my teachers and schoolmates thought I was slow because I had dyslexia, something built up in me that would do everything possible to avoid looking foolish.

Slowly, this crept into the community I was leading.

And I have to tell you, God couldn't really care less about whether I feel foolish. But he was *definitely* concerned about how my pride was affecting the community. So the breakthrough had to begin in my life first.

I promise you, if you create the space for the Lord to work in you first, if you slowly let that spread to the people you're closest to, if you grow that breakthrough into a communal swell, and if you do that, over and over again, you will build spiritual mass.

And you will have taught everyone around you how to do the same.

Suddenly, it's become repeatable, reproducible and multipliable.

A movement is beginning to swell.

PART 5
∽ THE CONCLUSION ∽

How, then, shall we live?

14

✷ TO EPHESUS ✷
AND BEYOND

Let's take one last look at the movemental center that Paul established in Acts 19.

Paul had gone from being a church planter with a team to a movement leader training movement leaders. Ephesus had enormous spiritual mass, and these movement leaders regularly orbited in and out of his *oikos*.

Later, when Paul wrote to the Ephesian church and all the churches planted out of it in eastern Asia—undoubtedly remembering his time there as he did—he said, "Our fight is not against flesh and blood. It's against the rulers, against the authorities, against the powers of this dark world and the spiritual forces of evil in the heavenly realms."[93] Clearly, Paul had created some commotion that stirred up the principalities, because they found their talons, their iron grip on the city, being loosened. When Paul saw a fundamental breakthrough in the city, he knew that there was a breach in the enemy's wall.

Now what he had come to do could be fully established in this community.

To understand the spiritual battle that was happening in Ephesus, we need to know a bit about the history of the city. Centuries before Paul ever darkened the doorstep of the city, some believe a black meteorite fell from the sky. Supposedly, when the people looked at it, they believed they could see the face of Artmeis, an important female deity of the Greek pantheon. In other cultures, she was known by other names.[94] Artemis was the goddess of wild

---

[93] Ephesians 6:12
[94] In Egypt, Isis. In the Roman Pantheon, Diana.

animals and the hunt. She was a protector to women, especially as virgins and in childbirth. As a femail deity, she symbolized the universal human need for provision and protection.

By the time Paul arrived, there was a massive industry surrounding her, including the largest building in the world, in which the image of Artemis was enshrined. Think Cowboys Stadium or Wembley Stadium big. It was a vast place that would be overwhelmingly impressive to anyone who visited.

The silversmiths, selling images of Artemis, were a marketing machine, and they had an economic engine attached to this figurehead of the city.

The seven sons of Sceva, whom we discussed earlier, had been casting out demons just using the name of Jesus, and it was working pretty well. But then they met a particularly powerful demon who beat them up and sent them running through the streets naked and bleeding.

That's what brought revival to this city! If the spiritual powers recognized the significance of Jesus, there must be something important happening.

People burned their demonic scrolls and things associated witchcraft and bowed their knee to Jesus. Their hearts were now open to the gospel. After Paul left, Timothy continued the work, developing the character and fiber of this sending center.

A few decades later, John the Apostle, the last disciple of Jesus still alive, brought Mary, the mother of Jesus, to live out her final days in this city. Church memory tells us that John, now an old man, saw all the idols of the city and went into the massive temple of Diana. He pointed at it and said, "I curse you in the name of Jesus," and it shattered. The Cult of Diana was removed and would never return in the form in which it had been known.

Ephesus had become the most important church in the world and had become a place of veneration and pilgrimage. At the First Council of Ephesus in the fifth century, the council agreed to a motion that Mary should be recognized as the mother of God, and thus hold a more exalted place among humans. Mary would become part of the faith equation.

A city that had once been in the stranglehold of a female deity once again found itself moving into captivity.

One minute the gospel was winning hands down, and the next it seems as though it was losing ground. Why? Because it's a Battle!

Paul's last chapter to these movemental churches was about spiritual warfare. This is real stuff, and it happens on the streets of your city as well. If you are going to be part of a Kingdom movement, you have to take seriously the role and reality of the principalities that stand against you.

Sometimes people talk about what's happening in their community and say, "It's like we're in a real battle right now."

There's no "like" about it. It's not "like" you're in a battle.

You're in a battle.

Now there is a lot of sketchy stuff out there on spiritual warfare. I always find it interesting that the things about which scripture is vague are the things about which some people feel the most certain. But one thing is for sure: the reality of the battle we are in is not something that scripture is ambiguous about.

We are at war, and you are going to get really hurt if you are not alert to the wiles of your enemy. He is an absolute *bastard*[95] and wants to see everything

....

[95] I do not use this word lightly. The visceral reaction you had when you read it points to the very nature of our enemy.

that you hold dear completely and utterly destroyed. He doesn't make truces. He doesn't have a soft spot in his heart. He wants to ravage your life and burn everything to the ground. He wants scorched earth.

It's interesting how James understood the way this works: "Submit to God, resist the enemy, and he will flee from you."[96]

Submission to God means putting him first, humbly listening for his voice. Then resist the Devil and say, "I am not moving," and he will flee from you. There is no talk of a great and epic sword fight or battering rams or arrows flying around. Submit to God. Stand your ground. He will flee.

That's how we win.

Paul emphasizes and explains this principle in Ephesians 6: "Put on all of the armor of God. It is yours and you have to wear it; it's covenant armor. Now having put it on and having laced up, this is what you do: **stand**."

STAND.

This idea of standing was a fundamental method of warfare that the Romans had used to conquer the world with their legions. "We have taken our stand, and we will not move." That's how the Romans won.

It was extraordinary. It wasn't sweeping battles. It usually had nothing to do with great strategy from a military genius. When the legions took the battlefield, they were an immovable object. The generals who built this machine trained their troops to do something that no one else did—the Roman Shield

....

[96] James 4:7

Wall. Before heavy artillery and mechanized armor were invented, Rome created the tank—basically, a square legion of soldiers with their shields locked together who were absolutely immoveable. In Latin it was called the *testudo*—the tortoise.

Rome won so many battles because their soldiers would not move in the battlefield. Like so many waves breaking on rocks, their enemies would crash up against the legion's shield wall and literally break themselves on it. So the Roman legions learned how to fight by standing still. They drew their enemies toward them, they stood still, and then when their enemies were killed on their shield wall, they took a step forward, making sure the people they walked over were properly dead, and waited for the next attack.

They didn't need to run. They simply needed to take one step at a time—one step more into enemy territory. Then another step. Shields locked together, many individuals working as one. *This is the metaphor Paul was tapping into when he said, "And above all of these things… STAND!"*

You don't have to be very clever to win, and for me, that's a good thing! You just need to learn how to submit to God. Stand your ground, locking shields with your family of soldiers. And your enemy will flee from you.

THE LITTLE THINGS ADD UP

A few chapters ago, I told my story, particularly as it intersected with the story of Sheffield. Having read stories like it from other churches (whether current or from ancient times), I know it's easy to get lost in the rosy glow of the aftermath.

We know it wasn't easy. My story makes that much clear. But we can miss the little things that actually add up and make a difference. In any story, because you have a limited amount of time in a re-telling, you miss things and lose things. Things fall through the cracks of your memory, or they don't quite fit into how you're sharing it.

The same is true of the story of Sheffield.

There are things that people don't know about that, that while seemingly insignificant at the time, proved to be mile markers, harbingers, and linchpins for things to come. You don't see it at the time—only in hindsight does it become apparent. All you can do is be faithful and do the things you feel like God is asking you to do.

I say this because I don't want that to be lost in the shuffle.

I don't want you to walk away from this book thinking what I'm sharing is prescriptive, like somehow you now have a formula for a Kingdom movement because you read some pages in a book.

The big things we stumbled on aren't divorced from the small things happening over and over again.

What you don't know is that for several years during the season of Lent, I returned to carrying that big heavy cross. This time, it was around the streets of Sheffield instead of the streets of Brixton Hill. This proved to be a rallying point for many in our community. We didn't do this forever, but we did it for a season.

What you don't know is that for many years, our team gathered five times a day for prayer, keeping the monastic prayer hours so that discipline, prayer, and love would saturate our team and our community. We didn't do this forever, but we did it for a season.

What you don't know is that when I left, the pastor who replaced me and a small band of compatriots (including their spouses and small children) felt called to give away all of their income for six months. They had a place to live, they had faith that God would provide, and that was it. They gave away every cent. They told no one about this. God not only provided, but did so in miraculous ways. What these young leaders learned provided just enough daylight so that a massive breakthrough poured out of this experience for the whole community. They didn't do this forever, but they did it for a season.

There are hundreds and hundreds of stories like these.

There is not a prescriptive way of understanding how to create and help lead a Kingdom movement. There is no magic formula in the sky. These stories? They won't be your story. God will ask you to do different things that reflect what he needs to do in your life, in the life of your specific community, and in your particular city.

We've shared some principles of what we've learned in our journey; hopefully, they will serve you in that to which the Lord has called you. But at the end of the day, here is what I've learned: at any given moment, I want to know what my Father is saying to me, and what he is saying to our community, and I want to respond in loving obedience.

There may be things he asks that I do for the rest of my life; there may be things that I do for only a season. But I keep returning to this question.

What is God saying to me, and what am I going to do about it?

The story of Sheffield? The stories I've just shared in this chapter? That's all they are. In many ways, we stumbled into something much bigger than ourselves, but we found it because we took the words of Jesus at face value and consistently asked ourselves those two questions over and over and over again.

What is God saying?

What am I going to do about it?

I can give you principles, I can't give you a prescription. What principles? UP, IN, OUT. Always live this way in your life and the life of your family. Building on this, develop a community marked by Passionate Spirituality, a Radical Community, and a Missional Zeal.

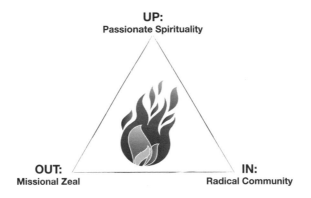

UP:
Passionate Spirituality

OUT:
Missional Zeal

IN:
Radical Community

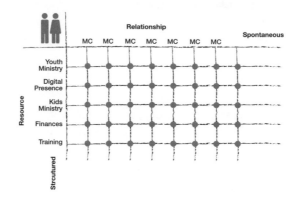

What principles? Build with relationships and resources that are capable of being spontaneous and structured.

What principles? Establish an extended family on mission as soon as you can.

What principles? Make disciples who make disciples by training them to answer two questions: "What is God saying?" "What are you going to do about it?"

Are those the only principles? Well, there are others contained in this book—so clearly there are more! Are there principles you need to add as you discover them? Without a doubt.

THE TWO FUNDAMENTAL QUESTIONS OF CHRISTIAN SPIRITUALITY:
What is God saying to me and what am I going to do about it?

Those of us involved in movemental leadership are still learning, still patiently observing what God is repeatedly doing. So yes, it's messy sometimes. But the movement I'm a part of with many others is changing the world, and I want to be in it—however ill-equipped I may be. I want to be there serving, leading where God sees fit, doing whatever I can to see the movement of God's Kingdom advance. At times, it's quite hard.

But I wouldn't be anywhere else because this is where I find my family, my mission and my Lord.

And I want you to come join us in this movemental renewal of all things.

So as you consider what it means for you to lead Kingdom movements, you don't need to remember every principle or example in this book. Hopefully, some will help you, but that's not the point.

The point is for you to ask God how he wants to use you in his movement, and to follow him in whatever way He leads.

And I believe that when you do, God will use you to make disciples who make disciples. He will use you and your *oikos* in his mission. And he will lead your *oikos* toward becoming a red-hot center that sends missional leaders out and welcomes them to orbit back in.

The little things will add up, and I trust that many centers of mission—like Jerusalem, like Antioch, like Ephesus, and even like Sheffield—are still to come.

The world is aching to be changed. It's begging for it. Will you help change it?